Publishing Children's Poetry For 19 Years

Giving verse a voice

The East & West Midlands
Edited by Jenni Bannister & Mark Richardson

First published in Great Britain in 2010 by:

 Young**Writers**

Young Writers
Remus House
Coltsfoot Drive
Peterborough
PE2 9JX
Telephone: 01733 890066
Website: www.youngwriters.co.uk

All Rights Reserved
Book Design by Spencer Hart, Ali Smith & Tim Christian
© Copyright Contributors 2010
SB ISBN 978-1-84924-840-2

Contents

Salma Riaz (12) 1

Brockampton Primary School, Worcester
Matthew Perry-Baker (10) 1
William Foxcroft (10) 2
Poppy Lane (9) 3
Lily McNamara (9) 3
Rebecca Dawson (10) 4
Isabel Benbow (10) 4
Bonnie Lewis (11) 5
Dylan Phillips (10) 5
Tom Hutchinson (10) 6
Henry Genner (9) 6
Jack Oliver (10) 7
Danielle Whiteley (10) 7
Lauren Powell-Bateson (10) 8
Zackery Biddle (10) 8

Campion School, Northampton
Hannah Whelan (14) 9
Olivia Partridge (14) 10
Eleanor Ward (13) 11
Chantal Roberts (14) 12
Alice Moore (11) 13
Daniella Day (13) 14
Michael Herd (12) 14
Evie Russell (13) 15
William Pearson (13) 15
Matthew Moore (12) 16
Laura Watkins (11) 16
John Leyden (11) 17
Mathew Price (11) 17
Amber May Rawlins (12) 18
Danielle Darlington (11) 18
Bryony Mead (12) 19
Alice Bagniuk (11) 19
Abigail Ashby (11) 20

Derby High School, Derby
Siobhan Bevan 20
Supreet Johal (11) 21
Lauren Moses (11) 22
Naomi Gleeson (11) 22
Mia Hudson (11) 23

Haven High Technology College, Boston
Lauren McLean (12) 23
Bethany Hardstaff (11) 24
Hannah Pryor (12) 24
Mikyla Skye Potton (11) 25
Cameron Chapman (11) 25
Darcie-Jane Beecham Bradley (12) 26
Lewis Cook (11) 26
Kai Kerbel (11) 27
Ann-Marie Clarke (13) 27
Aimee Davies (11) 28
Rosie Walker (11) 28
Sarah Jane Dawson (11) 29
Nathan Phillips (11) 29
Jason Jackson (12) 30
Jon Mannion (11) 30
Patrick Russell (11) 31
Lorna Richardson (11) 31
Jordan Mooney (12) 32
Krystal Dales (11) 32
Lauren Stephens (11) 33
Rebecca Shaw (11) 33
Ellie-Beth Capps (12) 34
Courtney Louise Hunt (11) 34
Jordan Histed-Palmer (11) 34
Dominic Goddard (12) 35
Jennifer Chan (11) 35
Cahlia Ross (11) 35
Travis Portas (11) 36
Pritiya Chowdhury (11) 36
James Carr (11) 36
Thomas Hall (11) 37
Danielle Eaton (11) 37
Sam McMahon (12) 37
Danielle Revell (11) 38
Jasmine Odiamin (11) 38

Nikola Anna Urbaniak 38
Liam Adams (11) 39
Jack Oglesbee (12) 39
Sam Reed (12) 39
Ryan Brooks (11) 40
Jarod O'Callaghan (11) 40
Kaleigh Earth (11) 40
Cameron Marshall (11) 41
Luke De Vries (11) 41
Tyler Green (11) 41
Callum Skinner (11) 42
Shola Ackroyd (11) 42
Aaron Currie (11) 42
Jade Walsh (11) 43
Jake Hall (11) 43
Lucy Marriott (11) 43
Katy Pearce (11) 44
Vicky Bell (11) 44
Thomas Bedford (11) 44
Amber Walsh (11) 45
Lauren Limb (11) 45
Toni Pragnall (11) 45
Cally Bagley (11) 46
Paige Dunworth (12) 46
Liam Green (12) 46
Kirsty Simons (12) 46

Highfields School, Matlock
William Hartley (12) 47
Chloe Wragg (11) 47
Leigh Hays (11) 48
Michaela Oldfield (12) 48
Emily Smith (11) 49
Hayley Smith (11) 49
Charlie Henderson-Howat (11) 49

Hillcrest School, Birmingham
Saghar Abdolseyed (11) 50
Esraa Rofaydaa Mohamed (14) 51
Aniqah Silvera (13) 52
Emily Baker (13) 53
Matilda Sandi (11) 54
Mariam Jan (13) 55
Sonal Patel (13) 56
Hope Fields (12) 57

Tamelia Harris (14) 58
Charlotte Smith (13) 59
Hibaq Mohamed (11) 60
Mahdi Rahman (11) 60
Shohanna Nashay Newman Kidd (11) ... 61
Melissa Louise Albutt (15) 61
Abeera Ali (12) 62
Billy-Jean McDonnell (14) 62
Sharna Hazell (11) 63
Larissa Shaw (14) 63
Silvia Cheza (13) 64
Sherene Lian O'Saye (12) 64
Aalyah Malcolm (12) 65
Yanci Vangua (15) 65
Sathvir Kaur (11) 66
Chadene Skerritt (13) 66
Nykola Buttress (13) 67
Deborah Smith (12) 67
Razan Adi (12) 68
Sameera Ali (12) 68
Maina Sandi (11) 69
Hirra Chohan (12) 69
Sara Ahmed (11) 70
Lauren Emma Dyson (14) 70
Kimiya Farjadifar (12) 71
Rumesha Baig (11) 71
Tameka Hemans (12) 72
Crystal King (14) 72
Alisha Aggrey (12) 73
Hillery Phillip (11) 73
Zohal Marofi (13) 74
Naila Khan (11) 74
Lucy Need (14) 75
Tamara Albutt (14) 75
Rhiannah Elaine Blake (12) 76
Amandeep Kaur Behal (13) 76
Marian Toko Zolana (13) 77
Lavin Mahmoud (14) 77
Arusa Mahmood & Bukky Ajayi (11) 78
Aisha Amhar (13) 78
Tanzeela Bi Hussain (12) 79
Shantella Palmer (14) 79
Chayonne Lee-Rondelle (13) 80
Ahliya Hussain (12) 80
Nashwa Bayan (12) 81

Rahma Abdi Osman (13) 81
Jasmin Gill (11) 82
Maimoonah Batool (11) 82
Kaprhys Lee-Bryan (12) 83
Sarah Megan Johnson (13) 83
Princess Bogle (15) 84
Aaliyah Spence (15) 84
Luanda Holness (13) 85
Divine Maguraushe (13) 85
Simran Kaur Chahal (12) 86
Kamohelo Modipa (12) 86
Kiran Singh Sole (12) 87
Damilola Ola (11) 87
Ammaarah Ali (11) 88
Keanne Bryan-Hakeem (13) 88
Sarah Abdoun (12) 89
Rene Nembhard (12) 89
Imaani Mitchell (11) 90
Sahar Saffari (12) 90
Destiny Williams (13) 91
Aleena Mahmood (13) 91
Mercedes Cunningham (11) 92
Roché Campbell (11) 92
Catherine Fadashe (14) 93
Michelle Cheung (12) 93
Connie George Alice Hackley (12) 94
Khianne Sherelle Nelson (13) 94
Patricia Tamayem (11) 95
Alana Campbell (13) 95
Deneshae Thomas (11) 96
Chardaya Daka (12) 96
Kamika Ferguson (13) 96
Jade Loxton (11) 97
Seraphina Codner Okundaye (13) 97
Sian Mills (12) 97
Chante Austin (12) 98
Rochelle Cranstoun (12) 98
Kirsty Ellikers (12) 98

King Edward VI Camp Hill School for Girls, Birmingham
Hayley Cross (12) 99
Akanksha Anand (12) 100
Bethany Evans (13) 101

Lees Brook Community Sports College, Derby
Elina Bannister (13) 101
Daniel William Buckley (15) 102
Jodee Leszczyszak (13) 102
Jordan Brewin (13) 103
Lauren Beavis (13) 103
Gavon Toor (13) 104
Peggy Watkins (12) 104
Daniel Dabbs (13) 105
Jordan Wynne (14) 105
Harvey Redfern (13) 106
Rebecca Helm (11) 106
Dina Harrison (13) 107
Sophie Jarman (11) 107
Tye Booker (12) 107
Rosie Hatton (11) 108
Callum Holler (13) 108
Megan Lambert (11) 108
Tegan Stacey (14) 109
Megan Frost (11) 109
Jordan Makulow (13) 109
Kelsey Hughes (11) 110
Michael-Thomas Percy (13) 110
Georgina Bruce (11) 110
Lauren Welsh (11) 111
Daniel Atkins (11) 111
Benjamin Smith (11) 111

Manor Park Community School, Nuneaton
Bradley Paul Steptoe (12) 111
Melanie Norton (11) 112
Dylan Bloore (11) 112
Keeley Michelle Harding (12) 113
Lauren Grantham (11) 113
Megan Karsten (11) 114
Rhys Jones (11) 114
Carly Jackson (12) 115
Declan Lloyd (11) 115
Andrew Barton (11) 116
Siannon Garrett (11) 116
Keira Jones (12) 117
Nicole Louise Jacques (11) 117
Sorrel Sutton (12) 118

Anil Gurung (12)	118
Jade Hildreth (12)	119
Shannon Jade Hughes (11)	119
Nicola Jayne Lenton (11)	120
Heather Jackson (11)	120
Alisha Dean (11)	121
Lily May Ellis (11)	121
Leah Crutchlow (12)	121
Dannii Paige Evans (11)	122
Owen Rogers (11)	122
Mason Steptoe (12)	122
Chelsea Hogarth (13)	123
Alice Kimberlin (11)	123
Kimberley Norton (12)	123
Arbaz Khalifa Faruk (12)	124
Thomas McIlveen (12)	124
Curtis Atkins (11)	124
Ashley Tuck & Leah Crutchlow (12)	125
Chelsea Chamberlain (12)	125
Lauren Jodie Beech (11)	125
Paige Smillie Blake (12)	126
Liam Jay Perry (11)	126
John James Gordon (11)	126
Siddiqah Khalifa (12)	127
Daniel Chandler (11)	127
James Wilson (12)	127
Mason Holligan (12)	128
Callum Twigger (12)	128
Georgia Leech (11)	128
Daniel King (12)	129
Jordon Blount-Hunt (12)	129
Ashley Tuck (12)	129
Naeem Ahmedabadi (12)	130
Caitlin Suzanna Lyons (12)	130
Ryan Mceachran (11)	130
Cara Wallace (12)	131

Prince Henry's High School, Evesham

Lauren Pritchard (13)	131
Joseph Robinson (13)	132

St Bede's Catholic Middle School, Redditch

Sophie Willmore (11)	132

Liya Tom (12)	133
Zack Nixon (12)	134
Tammi Richards (12)	135
Zoe McGahey (12)	136
Sara Rafaty (12)	137
Grace Down (11)	137
Charlie Evans (12)	138
Daniel Wilkinson (12)	138
Jack Bowen (12)	139
Jordon Dance (12)	139
Rebecca Hinks (12)	140
Chantelle Maher (12)	140
Chelsea Wilkes (12)	141
Jade Yarranton (12)	141

St Philip Howard RC School, Glossop

Adele Critchlow (13)	142
Lucy Aspden (13)	142
Jack Swift (13)	143

Springwell Community School, Chesterfield

Iris Hawkins (11)	143
Paige Holmes (11)	144
Liam Deane (11)	144
Olivia Bulley (11)	145
Ben Carley (11)	145
Amy Turner (12)	146
Katie Milner (11)	146
Esme Jones (11)	147
Kate Plowman (13)	147
Megan Lilley (13)	148
Benjamin Hall (13)	148
Lee-Anne Longmore (13)	148
Ryan Smith (13)	149
Ellie May Palmer (13)	149
Carl Jabes Leadbeater (13)	149

Swanwick School & Sports College, Swanwick

Joshua Messer (13)	150
Eva Shepherd (12)	150
Keiran Daken (14)	151
David Beavan (14)	151

The Poems

Success

As you may feel success is not for you,
Success is something special,
Which lasts a day or two.

Success can spread to everyone,
Everyone but you,
We may not realise that success is even in the sun.

You may think success is rare
And not in what you do,
But please do realise, that success is there in everything you care.

Although sometimes success we may not gain,
Success may be taking a holiday,
Away from the horrid rain.

Please do remember that I think too,
Success can last forever,
Not just a day or two.

Salma Riaz (12)

Avenbury River

Deep parts, shallow parts
The winding river pebbly and sandy,
Let your dogs loose.
Climb the trees, dangle over
Watch the sparkling water glistening in the sun
Watch kids play in the river
Two bridges to watch the water trickle through the rocks.
Don't get caught in the water grass
Murky water, see through water dripping from the trees.
Get your wellies on, but don't get freezing toes,
It scrapes away the bank, flooding is a problem,
The winding river and slippery banks.
Make the fields good for crops,
Wood sticks and stones fun to play with
Skimming stones on the water, catching sticks
Avenbury, the best river in the world!

Matthew Perry-Baker (10)
Brockampton Primary School, Worcester

Race To The Mountain (Wave Version)

Ready, steady, flow!
And off they go,
Wave No 1 I have a head start, crashing down that river.
Pounding and thrashing
Wave 1 is splashing,
The wave frothy,
The mud is like toffee
Pulling that wave right back.
But look wave 1 has turned its course,
Into the reservoir,
Down the drain!
Into the tap, now the cup
Trickling into the mouth
Glistening in the toilet,
But that has stopped
It's splashing through the sewers
And out to sea.

We haven't been keeping up with wave 2,
He's gone to the cold side of the mountain,
Look, he's frozen, he's got ten seconds or he'll be disqualified
Ten, nine, eight, seven, six, five, four, three, two, one,
Disqualified.
Back to wave 1, he's evaporated
Travelling to Iceland!
Round the volcano,
Back to Scotland.
He's completed the course
He can't stop.
The person who planned can't be clever
We haven't noticed
It's a *water cycle!*

William Foxcroft (10)
Brockampton Primary School, Worcester

Autumn Times

Autumn time is coming,
Winds whistling and blowing,
Leaves gather in small stumpy heaps,
Park wardens wandering aimlessly,
In these cold autumn times.

Hedgehogs nestling down,
Eating all they can,
Doing hardly anything else,
Going into piles of leaves,
Curling up in time for winter's reach.

Squirrels spending days gathering nuts,
Burying them and putting them into hollows,
Only to lose them next spring,
Quarrels with neighbours over whose nuts are whose?
Go on and on and on,
Till squirrel memories forget.

Crispy leaves floating down,
Brown, purple and orange sometimes,
Tree branches empty,
Except for evergreens.

Autumn's almost through now,
Winter coming fast,
Soon no more squirrels coming out,
Hedgehogs snuggled up too,
Goodbye from autumn,
Till next year.

Poppy Lane (9)
Brockampton Primary School, Worcester

The Beast

He creeps around the town with
His eyes yellow and bright.
He scares all of the children
As he stomps through the night.

Lily McNamara (9)
Brockampton Primary School, Worcester

Snow

I could see the snow falling
Through the school window
Everything was quiet
All the children going home
Myself, left all alone
I started to shiver
In my panic
I ran all the way home

The snow was melting
Into cold water
It was a dreaded day, week, year

The trees were shivering
The water was dripping
The animals were hiding away
The day was cold
The sky was dull
It felt like everything was still
I carried on walking
Until I could walk no more
Then I would sit down
And watch the clouds go by
The snow was all gone.

Rebecca Dawson (10)
Brockampton Primary School, Worcester

The Stream

The stream starts on a hill
And down it flows and sometimes it is still
It goes on forever and swirls round rocky pools
Crashing over the waterfall with a roar
Splashing onto the rocks more and more
Then it flows into the sea
And there it stays, merrily.

Isabel Benbow (10)
Brockampton Primary School, Worcester

The Ocean

If I could play in the
Ocean I would:

Swim with the
Jumping dolphins,

Dance with the
Turquoise jellyfish,

Eat with the
Majestic sharks,

I would sleep with
The goldfish, *shh,*

Play with the
Splashing starfish,

Walk in the
Crashing, smashing
Waves,

That is what I would
Do in the blue ocean.

Bonnie Lewis (11)
Brockampton Primary School, Worcester

Water

The sparkling waterfall,
Dropping down to the sea.
The sound of the dripping water,
Washing itself.
The dribbling rain,
Splashing onto the floor.
The sound of the flowing stream,
Travelling down to the sea.
As I look at the sea,
The sound washes through
My ears.

Dylan Phillips (10)
Brockampton Primary School, Worcester

Our World

The day becomes night,
Look up to the sky,
Where the beautiful stars roam.
We live on Earth,
The glorious Earth,
For the Earth is our wonderful home.

From Earth we can view,
The stars in the sky,
The best thing the Earth can provide.
It's greatest from a telescope,
I have one at home,
Looking up from Earth, the great big dome.

It carries on,
The Earth I mean,
For it never comes to an end.
One thing I don't understand,
Is you never know,
What's just around the bend.

Tom Hutchinson (10)
Brockampton Primary School, Worcester

The Planet Poem

Whirling, twirling around the sun,
Nine planets flying through space.
Faster than a man can run,
You'd think it was a race!

There's Mercury and Venus
And Earth and then there's Mars.
There's Jupiter and Saturn
And lots and lots of stars!

I think I've left out Uranus
And Neptune and Pluto.
There are also many moons out there
And rockets zooming to and fro!

Henry Genner (9)
Brockampton Primary School, Worcester

My River

Rivers that flow,
Rivers that are slow,
Rivers that are quiet,
That are never quick.
As I saw my face reflecting in my river,
It challenged me to a race,
As I looked at my competitor,
I saw my deserving face,
Did it wink back at me?
Rivers that flow,
Rivers that are slow,
Rivers that are quiet,
That are never quick.
Now, as I remembered my river as an old man,
I also remembered that the race continued on,
As I grew older,
This was about my river.

Jack Oliver (10)
Brockampton Primary School, Worcester

Thunderstorm

I could see the rainclouds in the distance
Closer and closer they came
The water came crashing down
The town was drowning in rain.

The thunderclouds were roaring
The sun was lazy and aloof
Pitter-patter rain was trickling down
Harder and harder the rain smashed
On the dark slate roof.

The sky was a gloomy, mysterious grey
It was a horrible day
Suddenly there was a strike of lightning!
Could it get more frightening?

Danielle Whiteley (10)
Brockampton Primary School, Worcester

Snow

The snow falls to the floor
Creating a cosy white blanket
I fall into the snow onto its soft mattress
And make an angel with my arms and legs.

Snowflakes shimmer in the night
And some are still in mid flight
This world changes into another
A crystal white wonderland.

Snowflakes crunch under my feet
They fall onto the trees like icing cakes
Silently falling to the ground
Not making a sound.

Lauren Powell-Bateson (10)
Brockampton Primary School, Worcester

If I Was To Sail On The Sea

If I was to sail on the sea
These are the things that I might see:
Fish and seaweed
Rocks and shells
Smashing water

Ocean smells
Hunt with sharks
Seagulls fly
Above the sky
Up there high.

Zackery Biddle (10)
Brockampton Primary School, Worcester

Hatred

The CO_2 is building up,
The fossil fuels burn out.
There simply is just not enough
Clean air to go about.
The wars are tearing us apart,
The guns are shooting rounds
The bombs explode so loudly,
But we die without a sound.
Every morning on the news,
There's cruelty, hate and fear,
We pray nothing has happened to
The ones that we hold dear.
Child abuse and pet neglect,
Nobody escapes it.
It hangs around - a murky fog
The feeling we call hatred.
In foreign countries, people starve,
World debt is in a muddle.
It's 'money this' and 'money that'
A power hungry struggle.
Drugs infect communities,
Like a bad disease.
Respect goes out the window
And kids do what they please.
The issues like world hunger
May take a while to fix.
But saying 'please' and 'thank you'
Are very easy tricks.
If everybody had a laugh
And we all cracked a smile,
The world would light with happiness,
Just for a little while
Land and sea, day and night,
These things were made to last.
But hate's gone by its sell-by date,
Let's put it in the past.

Hannah Whelan (14)
Campion School, Northampton

Tomorrow

Yesterday I was African,
Today I am black . . .
Today I was sold,
Tomorrow I'll sell,
Thinking of freedom
Away from this Hell.
Today I am beaten,
Tomorrow I'll win
Using my strength
Cos the colour of my skin.
Today I'm in rags,
Tomorrow in silk
Like the arrogant white men
Skin coloured like milk.
Today I have wounds,
Tomorrow just scars
Laid in the dirt
Under the stars.
Today how I hurt,
Tomorrow I'll smile,
This pain will soon go,
It'll just take a while.
Today I'm an animal,
Tomorrow a man
As I think about the railroad,
My escape route plan.
Today I am starving,
Tomorrow I'm fed,
My friend Zephaniah
Is whipped till he's dead.
Today I feel shameful,
Tomorrow with pride,
My hopes and my dreams
I won't have to hide.
Today I've no mind,
Tomorrow a soul,
Time's running out
Being free is my goal.

Today I will scream,
Tomorrow my dream,
This horrible nightmare
Will never have been.
Today I am chained,
Tomorrow I'm free . . .

Olivia Partridge (14)
Campion School, Northampton

The Reign Of The Knife

I'm sat here at home,
Staring at the door.
One wrong step and
Who knows what's in store.

Down on the street
Playing with a mate.
We hear them coming
Through the estate.

We run in fear,
Not wanting to know,
How a group of wolves,
Will attack a doe.

We hear their laughter
From our hiding place
The scream then follows, with
The horror on their face.

Their footsteps thump,
As they run away.
The knife now red,
Next to its prey.

Nothing will happen
It's just life
The gangs and violence
The reign of the knife.

Eleanor Ward (13)
Campion School, Northampton

Breaking The Mould

They've broken the mould
But they're not different
Who's to say they're not normal?
They like the same sex,
So what if they do?
You like the opposite sex,
Does that mean you're different?
You're not normal?
No!
They've broken the mould
So why hassle them?
They do nothing to you
They don't have a disease
So why run from them?
Why call them names?
Why?
They've broken the mould
But they're just like you
They have the same feelings.
They do the same things
They have a good laugh
They love one another
So are they really different?
They know you should love a person
Not a man or a woman
They've broken the mould.

Chantal Roberts (14)
Campion School, Northampton

The Cold, Cruel World

As the TV chatters on,
About the world,
The cold, cruel world.

We live in it,
We sleep in it,
We eat in it!

It goes on about the world today,
The litter is still piling up,
Still the world won't change!

We live in it,
We sleep in it,
We eat in it!

We're all going to die in pain,
They said it won't be nice,
They said we will pay!

We live in it,
We sleep in it,
We eat in it!

And still the TV chatters on,
About the world,
The cold, cruel world.

Alice Moore (11)
Campion School, Northampton

Let Me Be

Taunting, teasing, when will it end?
All I need is a kind word, a friend.
Someone please, reach out your hand,
I'm just like you! Don't you understand?

Is this normal? How can it be?
When people do this to someone like me.
I'm not a villain, not unkind,
So why can't I live without being defined?

I can't go out, can't walk down the street,
Children as young as six taught how to beat!
It's me they're after, leave me alone!
Why am I confined like an animal to my home?

Why should it matter? The colour of my skin,
In this cruel world, we will never win.
Crying, dying, no one cares,
Pelted with rocks, given evil glares.

Maybe sometime it will be OK,
My mum and dad will be free to live today.
Someone, somewhere will turn around and say,
They've done nothing wrong, they don't need to pay!

Daniella Day (13)
Campion School, Northampton

The Children Of War

We are the children of war,
Our pain and misery echoes in the wind,
We feel about this war, we feel about sins,
We don't care about this war as much as we think,
But the anger of both sides share a link.

The drums of war beat again,
They are hurt on the outside, we are hurt in,
The anger and hurt will begin once more,
The misery is sinful, we all feel the pain.

Michael Herd (12)
Campion School, Northampton

Everyday Silence

Everyday silence, walking down the street
All that I can hear, is the stomping of my feet.
Everyday silence, as I enter my school
Why are they so mean to me, I know I'm not that cool.

Everyday silence, sitting in the class
I sit staring through the window's glass.
Everyday silence, after break time
I always seem to be, the first in line.

Everyday silence, in ICT
Although I don't ask, no one sits next to me.
Everyday silence, in the canteen
No one would hear me, even if I could scream.

Everyday silence, seeing all the friends
What is this feeling? Please tell me how it ends.
Everyday silence, I'm always alone
So next time you ring my doorbell, I won't be home.

Evie Russell (13)
Campion School, Northampton

Stuck In The Middle

I am an average boy, with a decent life
With a nice dad, who has a nice wife
But away from prying eyes, at the dawn of the night
When I'm up in my bed, my parents turn out the lights
A barrage of words, can be audibly heard
Up the stairs to my room, where I quiver like a bird
It is like Britain and Germany, are at it again
And I am enclosed, when the clock is at ten
The war of the words, is scaring me stiff
My sister is oblivious, but I could jump off a cliff
Now I must carry on and still stay strong
While stuck in the middle, of this battle long
So that is me, fully covered
I'm really worried about the future
But it's not up to me, as I'm just stuck in the middle.

William Pearson (13)
Campion School, Northampton

Crime

Crime is unforgivable,
In every way possible.
Crime is just horrible,
Piercing the inside.

Why on earth do we have to suffer,
Just for the heartless people?
Why do we open the door to the
People who we know cause this mess?

We watch the news every day
And hear about someone who was stabbed and passed away.
We listen to the sirens every day
Rushing to the scene of a mean attack.

Crime is unforgivable,
In every way possible.
Crime is just horrible,
Piercing the inside.

Matthew Moore (12)
Campion School, Northampton

Family . . .

Family . . . everyone says they're the best thing!
I say I have to disagree
I would rather play out and stay out late
Then sit with them watching TV.

Family . . . why do they never understand?
Mum has no fashion sense
And Dad just watches TV
My brother who I never see
And my dog that's barking mad!

Why can't I have a normal family
Like everybody else?
Family . . . even though you're all mad
I have to agree, you're something special
And that's that!

Laura Watkins (11)
Campion School, Northampton

Global Warming

Why don't people hear the warning?
All about global warming
Why can't they hear it now?

Can't they see what is forming?
When the layers are falling,
Why can't they hear it now?

Can't they see the clouds are storming?
Now it's getting annoying
Why can't they hear it now?

People go eco-friendly
Rather than going deadly
Why can't they do it now?

Why don't people hear the warning?
All about global warming
Why can't they hear it now?

John Leyden (11)
Campion School, Northampton

War, Crime And Abuse

One night we were watching the news
It was all about war, crime and abuse
I said, 'Why do things happen like this?'
They answered, 'I don't know, it is just the way it is.'

Down in Afghanistan
There is a war
I feel very sorry
As they are so poor.

One night we were watching the news
It was all about crime and abuse
I said, 'Why do things happen like this?'
They answered, 'I don't know, it is just the way it is.'

Down every street there is a crime.

Mathew Price (11)
Campion School, Northampton

You're A Joke

I wish that cool people,
Would just accept me for who I am
And not just disregard me, 'cause I'm not like them.
Just because I don't drink or smoke,
Doesn't mean I'm not as cool,
If I was to drink or smoke, I guess I'd be a fool!
So, why judge me because I'm not like you?
Just coz I don't like the things you do?
People are just people, different or the same!
So if you think I'm not as cool as you, then who is it to blame?
Should I change myself for you?
Or change myself for me?
Coz if I'm not as cool as you
Because I don't drink or smoke,
Then I'd best not be friends with you
Coz that makes you a joke!

Amber May Rawlins (12)
Campion School, Northampton

Celebrities

Life of luxury, life of fame;
Life of glory, life of shame,
Life of a celebrity.
Life of bleaching, life of TV;
Life of money, life of iced tea,
Life of a celebrity.
Life of Grammies, life of expense;
Life of feeling, life of suspense,
Life of a celebrity.

So why do they get special treatment?
Why do they think they're the best?
Because we're all human beings,
We're the same as all the rest!

Danielle Darlington (11)
Campion School, Northampton

Don't Do It!

Please don't pull my hair,
Please don't take my chair.
Please don't annoy me,
Please don't hurt me.
I'm tired, I'm annoyed,
Please don't . . .

Please don't sing in my ear,
Please don't come over here.
Please don't whisper about me,
Please don't copy me.
I'm tired, I'm annoyed,
Please don't!

Bryony Mead (12)
Campion School, Northampton

Let Them Live

If animals were people and you were them too,
How would you like it if they came and killed you?
Just for your hair
Or just for your skin?
Living alone, ill and distraught, no one cares whether you are or not,
It doesn't make sense how you could do it,
Hurt an animal and still live around it.
Being happy is what we all want,
But killing animals doesn't help them one bit.

You have your own life, family and friends,
Why take the life of a poor animal and use it against them?

Alice Bagniuk (11)
Campion School, Northampton

Bullying

Bullying is bad
Bullying is wrong
Bullying upsets people
Bullying makes them sad.

Imagine if you were being bullied
Imagine what it would feel like
Imagine if you were being called names
Imagine if you were being left out.

Think, think, you wouldn't like it . . .
So why do it!

Abigail Ashby (11)
Campion School, Northampton

Emotions

Feelings can be things you see every day,
A cold winter's night,
Or a warm sun's ray.

Happiness is a hot summer's day,
Laughs and smiles,
Ice cream while we play.

Sadness is a cold winter's night,
Afraid and alone,
Hope out of sight.

Love is precious, a graceful dove,
It needs two wings,
Can't fly with just one.

As you can see, there are emotions all around,
In the sea and the sky
And on the ground.

Siobhan Bevan
Derby High School, Derby

The Monkey

I'm a monkey
Sitting in the zoo
I'm a monkey
And I'm so sad.

I have no friends
And the other monkeys hate me.
And that's not all
I still have more.

They kick me
They punch me.
They poke me
Until a girl comes.

I'm a monkey
Sitting in the zoo.
I'm a monkey
And I'm so happy.

I have loads of friends
And the other monkeys love me.
And that is all
I have no more.

Although I love my girlfriend.

Supreet Johal (11)
Derby High School, Derby

What Feelings Mean To Me!

F riendship is like looking for gold,
   When you find it, you appreciate it.
E xcitement is like a tingling feeling,
   Bursting to get out.
E njoyment is like having the time
   Of your life.
L ove is like picking petals off a flower,
   Wishing that the answer would be 'they love me'.
I rritation is like a fly,
   Buzzing around in your head.
N eglected is like ignoring the most important
   Person in your life.
G ratefulness is like thanking someone,
   For saving your life.
S adness is like a heavy brick,
   Fixed inside you.

Lauren Moses (11)
Derby High School, Derby

The Right Result

Her face glaring
The colour red
You could see her anger
Running through her head

Then the tears came
Trickling down and down
Her skin was pale
Her eyebrows in a frown

Next was the smile
Her pearly whites showing
Her eyes were bright
And her skin was glowing.

Naomi Gleeson (11)
Derby High School, Derby

It's Going To Be A Bad Start

I have a feeling that's special to me,
It's been kept a secret for nobody to see,
Anticipation and worry as I entered the drive,
Slowly thinking, *will I survive?*
Scared, as people bustled everywhere,
Some even stopped to have a little stare,
Calm came over me pretty soon,
Fearless and confident as I entered the room,
Friends and chatting my worry went by,
This was my first day at Derby High.

Mia Hudson (11)
Derby High School, Derby

Cinderella

Sat in her cellar,
Watching the people go by,
But when she said, 'Hi!'
They thought she was weird,
Even the one with a beard.
A letter came one day, she didn't know what to say,
It was about a ball in the biggest ever hall,
So she said, 'What's up?'
Her stepmum came home
And stepsisters got out the shaving foam,
To shave their legs, put their clothes on pegs.
I couldn't go out, what a silly doubt,
When they left, I slammed doors,
Because I had to do the chores,
All I did was break some plates,
Then strangely, a fairy godmother came, I thought it was fate,
She said, 'Hello,' and then sat down below,
'Do you want to go to that ball in the biggest ever hall?'
Then strangely turned evil,
'No, I don't want to go to a stupid ball in a silly hall!
So get out of my house, or I'll get my mice friends out.'

Lauren McLean (12)
Haven High Technology College, Boston

Please Mummy

Please Mummy!
There are spiders in my bed
Don't let them gobble me up
Until I am dead.

But please Mummy!
I need a drink
But the only thing is, if I do
I might shrink.

Please, please Mummy!
I need a bath
But if I go in
Everyone will laugh.

Mummy! Mummy!
There are people out there
But the only problem is
I am very, very scared.

Mummy!
There's a really mean lad
And that's why
I am very, very sad.

Oh! Mummy!
I need a cuddle
Because it's dark outside
So give me a snuggle.

Bethany Hardstaff (11)
Haven High Technology College, Boston

Family Is Simply The Best!

F riendly people are always in your family
A re always there when you need a helping hand
M y family are simply the best!
I f you want a friend, just go to the best people you know, your family
L ove and protect each other
Y ou can always ask your family for help and support.

Hannah Pryor (12)
Haven High Technology College, Boston

Hallowe'en

Horrible black witches fly
Through the black midnight sky with glittering stars
All the other stay down on the grey, spooky ground,
While looking up at the midnight sky
With their grey cauldrons, with lots of orange pumpkins,
Lit with white candles inside
And lie the witches black and white, small spooky cat with a pink collar.
Lightning white stars shine through the midnight sky,
While the witches deliver their midnight fright
Orange pumpkins light up the gleaming dark, midnight sky
While the witches fly through the night,
Walking children going to the house
To get juicy sweets from the people.
Every child walks around the streets, knocking on doors.
Every child expects sweets and more
Night draws in, then it starts to be Hallowe'en
And every child gets dressed up for trick or treating
To get their delicious, juicy sweets from the door they knocked on.

Mikyla Skye Potton (11)
Haven High Technology College, Boston

Just Bored

Nothing is doing nothing
Bored, hungry
That's it, that's all I can think of

Looking for something to do
I walk up the stairs, play games
Even if that's boring too

I go to the park
Maybe then I won't be bored
But I am, I'm going home

Still bored, I walk back home
This is worse!
I'll just watch TV
Boring - just bored.

Cameron Chapman (11)
Haven High Technology College, Boston

Manchester Untied

M ovement
A ction
N ot divers
C ool
H appy
E xciting
S upportive
T he best
E verlasting
R eally goo

U ndefeated
N ever to fail
I maginative
T oo good
E nergetic
D extrous.

Darcie-Jane Beecham Bradley (12)
Haven High Technology College, Boston

Sport Basketball

S port is for everyone
P eople play all day long
O ver the night and through the day
R owing and riding all around
T ravelling and contact

B asket is the way to score
A nyone can score a basket, just get it through the net
S core all day through and don't stop
K eep playing and you will get better
E verybody jumps to score the basket
B all in your hands
A ll people like basketball, it's fun
L ike you will score, just ask how to play
L ovely times I will show you how to play
    Just come down to my house some day.

Lewis Cook (11)
Haven High Technology College, Boston

Going Out Of Assembly

Mrs Balley's class skipped gracefully back to class
Miss Frog's class leaped away,
Mr Cool's class moon-walked away,
Mrs Snake's class slithered past the rest,
Miss Boxer's class pounded their way out,
Mr Duncan's class didn't know what to do,
Mrs Car's class zoomed out,
Miss Water's class just
          T
             R
               I
                 C
                   K
                     L
                       E
                         D away.

Kai Kerbel (11)
Haven High Technology College, Boston

I Love You

I miss you when you're not around,
To keep my feet firmly on the ground,
I need to know if you see,
That you're definitely made for me.
I love to see you every day,
Do I really need to say,
That I support whatever you do,
Because I am truly in love with you.
I'm telling you just how I feel,
Because my heart is now spinning on a wheel,
You have the key into my heart,
Together we are a work of art.
You love me,
It's easy to see,
I know you do
And I love you too.

Ann-Marie Clarke (13)
Haven High Technology College, Boston

Today I Feel

Today I feel as:
Fit as a fiddle,
As hot as a griddle,
As bouncy as a ball,
As tall as a wall,
As high as a kite,
As strong as a bull,
Right as rain,
As warm as wool,
Chirpy as a chick
And as thick as sticks.

With a wiggle and a giggle
I feel so alive,
So what about you?
Do you feel alive?

Aimee Davies (11)
Haven High Technology College, Boston

Best M8s

Best m8s are there for you
And never let you down,
They say lovely comments,
Like you're wearing a nice gown.

Best m8s like you
And Courtney too,
Are always there for me,
When I'm sad,
Or feeling blue.

So there you go,
Best m8s are a flow,
They come and go,
So make it last; *yo!*

Rosie Walker (11)
Haven High Technology College, Boston

Please Friends!

Please Bethany
I need a friend
But if I don't, I won't mend

Please Bethany
I need some help
If I don't, it won't melt

Please Sarah
I need you
But if you don't, I will leave you

Please Sarah
We need to go
If we don't we will not sew.

Sarah Jane Dawson (11)
Haven High Technology College, Boston

Flying And Dying

Flying and dying, my family started crying
I flew and flew, that's what I did
I got a sketch pad and a toy car, that's what I drew
I looked in the sky at the stars to see
At the same time they twinkled at me
I like Harry Potter on his broomstick whilst watching a crow
flying high and low
I flew on my broomstick, going high and low
And then I fell off and killed the crow
The poor little crow flying high and low, the poor little crow
Was not alive, the little crow ended up in the glimpse of a glow
My family started crying that the crow was dying
But it wasn't my fault.

Nathan Phillips (11)
Haven High Technology College, Boston

Vampire Happy

Hallowe'en is coming nigh,
The costumes, *ugh!*
And the sweets,
They think they're a vampire,
Just like me.
But I know that's very wrong,
With toil, toil trouble,
I'm singing this like a poem,
Snake fangs,
Dragon fire,
Kerosene,
Teeth from the Jonas Brothers
And evil eyes.

Jason Jackson (12)
Haven High Technology College, Boston

Bullworth Battle

There was a boy called Jimmy,
Who was in a battle with the Jocks and bullies,
With the nerds and preps,
The Jocks took too many steps,
The nerds were done,
But the preps had just begun,
The bullies went down, one by one,
Jocks started having fun,
Jocks down, preps down,
Jimmy wore the crown,
The remaining Jocks swam away
And some used the doggy paddle,
That was the end of the Bullworth Battle.

Jon Mannion (11)
Haven High Technology College, Boston

My Little Pony, Donkey And Froggy

My little pony,
Skinny and bony,
It might be a phoney,
But it's my little pony!

My little donkey,
His legs are wonky,
It might change into a monkey,
But it's my little donkey.

My little froggy,
Ate my little doggy,
Now he's not my hobby,
I've turned him into a lobby.

Patrick Russell (11)
Haven High Technology College, Boston

Untitled

My name is Trevor
And I am so clever,
So don't mess with me,
'Cause I'll drown you in the sea!

My name is Fred
And I sleep in my bed,
It is so warm,
So I eat corn!

My name is Bob
And I am a blob,
I am a brat
And I am so fat!

Lorna Richardson (11)
Haven High Technology College, Boston

Underwater Rats

The underwater rats
Smell like dead cats
They walk around in leather jackets
And they love to eat crisp packets
Their favourite flavour is BBQ
And after that, they need the loo
Then they say that happens all the time
Instead of that we should have eaten that lime
One of the rats says we must be barmy
But shall we sing, because we're a perfect harmony?
That was the story of the three rats
Oh, my goodness! Where are those cats?

Jordan Mooney (12)
Haven High Technology College, Boston

Wild Horses Running Free

Wild they run free,
Galloping in the wide open spaces,
Rarely seen by the human eye,
Sometimes seen as pests,
Only those who understand them,
Truly see them for what they are,
When young, they are playful,
Then as they grow, they protect the herd
From the threats that lie in wait,
If one wanders they surely are doomed,
Unless their cunning, wits, speed
Can save them.

Krystal Dales (11)
Haven High Technology College, Boston

Nightfall

The trees are swaying, the bushes are blowing,
The lakes are stone still and the rivers are flowing,
The world in the wind, up in the sky,
The darkness is growing, it's nearly nigh,
Animals at home, wrapped up tight,
They shouldn't be out on this winter's night,
The figure in the tree flutters about,
'Is that an owl?' some may shout,
The eerie howl became a fright,
To the figure in the tree on that misty night,
The light approaches from the clouds,
Here comes the stampede of animals, in such crowds.

Lauren Stephens (11)
Haven High Technology College, Boston

Sister!

My little sis
She hates to hit and miss
I'm always the victim
She always eats a lot of vitamins
She has a very strong punch
I won't survive for lunch
She acts so innocent
Whilst she chews on her mint
Mum always believes her
I sit on my bed waiting for something to occur
Nothing ever appears in my mind
But it doesn't matter, even if she's not kind.

Rebecca Shaw (11)
Haven High Technology College, Boston

Tennis

T ension
E ncouraging
N oisy
N ow
I nstructing
S erious

I nvincible
S tomach aching

F un
U nconscious
N ew.

Ellie-Beth Capps (12)
Haven High Technology College, Boston

On The Way To School . . .

My ma said it's the golden rule,
To wear my seatbelt on the way to school.
I suppose she may be right,
Since I had a bad dream last night.

Cars crashing, screams screaming,
Hearts pumping, pressure rising,
Fires screeching, hearts bleeding,
And what a *bad* dream!
My ma sounded so keen.

Though my ma did say it was the golden rule,
To wear my seatbelt on the way to school.

Courtney Louise Hunt (11)
Haven High Technology College, Boston

Haiku

My name is Jordan
And my surname is Histed
I like to play sports.

Jordan Histed-Palmer (11)
Haven High Technology College, Boston

Wayne Rooney

W icked at football he is
A wesome but sometimes gets
Y ellow cards and he
N ever fights on the pitch and he trains hard
E very day for football, he doesn't get

R ed cards very
O ften because he doesn't get
O ut of control
N ormally, because he doesn't want to get banned
E very match because he loves playing football
Y et he is the best Manchester United player.

Dominic Goddard (12)
Haven High Technology College, Boston

Friends

When you are down with a frown
They will cheer you up, like a clown
The light of your friendship lasts forever, then
Through the darkness to the end.

They are there when you need them
They'll be there quicker than a growing stem
When you're at home, all alone
You can always catch them on the phone.

Friends are the ones that are there all alone
When feeling bad or singing a song!

Jennifer Chan (11)
Haven High Technology College, Boston

Mary Had A Little Lamb

Mary had a little lamb and called it Kabrina,
Then she did a little dance, now her name is Sabrina.
Then she did a dance again and landed in my pie,
Then my butcher came along and said that you must *die!*

Cahlia Ross (11)
Haven High Technology College, Boston

Summer

See the summer brightly shine,
Unless you look at it, you will go blind.
Mother, Mother, it's sunny outside,
Mother, Mother, I'm coming in.
I'm getting burnt outside,
Everywhere outside, it's sunny.
Running to my mother,
It's been a month since summer
And it's now winter,
Please come back summer!

Travis Portas (11)
Haven High Technology College, Boston

Hallowe'en Trouble!

H orrible witches flying through the sky
A utumn spells make people die
L ying on the floor waiting to get you
L ots of ghosts you'll never know what they'll do
O ver your head ghosts will flutter
W itches will eat bread with butter
E vil bats flutter up high
E ven when you don't know why
N ight is gruesome, night is mean
   Be careful what you do on Hallowe'en!

Pritiya Chowdhury (11)
Haven High Technology College, Boston

One Day In November

One day in November,
I am going to die,
Before I die, I will eat a pork pie,

One day in November,
I will fly
And I will be an angel in the sky.

James Carr (11)
Haven High Technology College, Boston

Food In My Kitchen

The smells in my kitchen smell like a rose
From the garden of youth
As I put the sausages in, they go *bang, pop, sizzle!*
I put in the bacon, I go *mmm* for what is cooking within.
The microwave goes *ping*
For the beans are done
It's gonna smell tonight
What a fright
Can't wait till tea
How much will there be?

Thomas Hall (11)
Haven High Technology College, Boston

My Loving Friends

I love my friends,
Even though they pinch my pens,
We sometimes have fall-outs,
But after all, they're my best friends,
Every day we hang around,
Not like monkeys that fall to the ground,
They're like my soulmates,
Who always walk me out the gates,
We always look out for each other,
My best friend for life is Nikita and she loves her baby brother.

Danielle Eaton (11)
Haven High Technology College, Boston

Fat Sam

F at Sam is a citizen of Pig Ville
A t Pig Ville his best friend was called Bill
T he town mayor was called Pat

S o as you can guess he was very fat
A lso the town postman
M ost of the time, he hit people with a frying pan.

Sam McMahon (12)
Haven High Technology College, Boston

Family

Mums are cool
Dads play pool
Sisters are lame
Brothers are the same
Uncles are loveable
Aunties are huggable
Nans are grotty
Grandads are snotty
Cousins make you smile
But most of all, I love my family.

Danielle Revell (11)
Haven High Technology College, Boston

Haikus

My name is Jasmine
I live in a cardboard box
And I like clubbing

My name is Jasmine
I love to eat Macky Dees
In my cardboard box

My name is Jasmine
Sadly, I can't get clever
Don't push the limit.

Jasmine Odiamin (11)
Haven High Technology College, Boston

My Friends Are Cool!

My friends are cool just like me,
As you can see, they just copy me.

We are all a gang
And we text in slang.

We go to places together
And we will be best friends forever!

Nikola Anna Urbaniak
Haven High Technology College, Boston

Hallowe'en - Haikus

Hallowe'en is close
Let's go trick or treating now
It's time to dress up

I love Hallowe'en
You'd better dress up scary
I get lots of sweets

Go out with your friends
Go and scare lots of people
Hallowe'en is fun!

Liam Adams (11)
Haven High Technology College, Boston

Jack Rulz

Jack has a pack of lies,
He always eats pies
Because he's a fatty bum, bum
He likes to suck his thumb, thumb.

Ryan is a good friend,
But he goes crazy at times,
Also he likes to climb,
He will help me to the end,
Because he's a good friend.

Jack Oglesbee (12)
Haven High Technology College, Boston

Ghosts

S melly old bones
A t Haven High
M eet all the ghosts at Haven High

R eed is going to get you
E at the food at Haven High, don't
E at the food at Haven High
D on't eat the food at Haven High.

Sam Reed (12)
Haven High Technology College, Boston

Random

The cat sat on the mat
Began to eat a rat
He got a little fat
He turned into Garfield
So he went to live in a big field

The cat sat on the mat
Decided to bury his head
He went to sleep without a peep
And didn't wake up till the morning.

Ryan Brooks (11)
Haven High Technology College, Boston

Mad Worlds

M an killing
A fter deaths
D eath and blood

W hite and black
O verhead kills
R ose thorn train
L ife-taking
D estruction
S napping necks.

Jarod O'Callaghan (11)
Haven High Technology College, Boston

All About Me

K aleigh is my name
A nd I have attitude
L ike eating chocolate
E very day with Paige
I ntelligent
G oing home from school, *yeah!*
H ome, home sweet home.

Kaleigh Earth (11)
Haven High Technology College, Boston

Hallowe'en

H allowe'en is a scary night
A nd vampires, bats and ghosts come out to fright.
L oads of pumpkins,
L ots of candy and sweets about.
O ff go the bright lights,
W ith candles alight in the night.
E veryone walking around,
E very creature in sight,
N ight-night, wait for the morning light.

Cameron Marshall (11)
Haven High Technology College, Boston

Hallowe'en

H appy kids are singing along
A lso adults screaming *bing-bong!*
L oud at times but not forever
L eeches are evil they also love feathers
O ften cool and sometimes scary
W erewolves are hungry and very hairy
E ven though we've got no sweets
E verlasting monster treats
N ight-time is here and the clocks strikes - *gong!*

Luke De Vries (11)
Haven High Technology College, Boston

Star Wars

S hips flying all the time
T ie fighters flying all over space
A grenade round every corner
R ebels are running round the bases

W ookies will win their wars
A ll droids will protect
R 2-D2 is on your back
S tar Wars is a battle never lost.

Tyler Green (11)
Haven High Technology College, Boston

Hallowe'en

H orrible witches fly in the sky
A ll the children are in their pie
L iking the children's meat to eat
L oving them on full heat
O wls give the sign of witches
W itches eat all the titches
E very night they come to fright
E ven if it is a bright night
N ever have witches been a sight.

Callum Skinner (11)
Haven High Technology College, Boston

A Scary Hallowe'en Night

H allowe'en is a night for fright
A lways witches in the ditches
L oads of people in the street
L ooking for something good to eat
O pen the door for a treat
W hy not give us a scary beat
E verywhere a scary sight
E ven werewolves in the night
N ever be scared, it's just a fright.

Shola Ackroyd (11)
Haven High Technology College, Boston

Star Wars Fight!

S tar fighters exploding in battle
T hermal detonators round every corner
A ttack cruisers moving through hyperspace
R obots run round Republic gunships

W ars on every planet that needs to be conquered
A ll rebellions win their wars
R epublic troops training to win their battles
S ith lords defeating Republic troops and Jedi knights.

Aaron Currie (11)
Haven High Technology College, Boston

Haunted Hallowe'en

H orrors
A cting
L oopy Lucy's coming
L iving dead
O n the road
W icked witches
E xcitingly
E ating sweets
N asty spells.

Jade Walsh (11)
Haven High Technology College, Boston

Hallowe'en

H orrible witches
A ll night long
L ots of frights
L ots of tricks
O n a broomstick
W hizzing through the sky
E veryone dressed up
E veryone getting sweets
N ever get scared.

Jake Hall (11)
Haven High Technology College, Boston

My Mate Mick

One day I bought a small pet mouse
And brought him home to my little cosy house,
He scared my dog
And ate a frog,
It made him go pale,
He was dragging his tail,
I called him Mick,
Because he kept being sick.

Lucy Marriott (11)
Haven High Technology College, Boston

Hallowe'en

H orrible haunted house
A wful ghosts and ghouls appear at night
L ate nights out
L ucky dip in their pots full of sweets
O rdering people to give you sweets
W icked witches cackling down the road
E ndeavouring the spirits
E verlasting nights
N o! Don't give me a fright!

Katy Pearce (11)
Haven High Technology College, Boston

Hallowe'en

H owling by the werewolves' pack
A ngry cries by the bodies in the sack
L eeches crawl and scatter in your hair
L imping zombies give you a scare
O wls swoop and steal your sweets
W impy grannies gives you some treats
E clispes night glows up red
E vil monsters under your bed
N ight-night, sleep tight, don't let the zombies bite!

Vicky Bell (11)
Haven High Technology College, Boston

My Animals

My little cats
One skinny and one fat
But also,
My little pony
He might be a phoney
And skinny and bony
He's my little pony.

Thomas Bedford (11)
Haven High Technology College, Boston

Hallowe'en

H orrible witches flying
A round all night
L aughing while the children scream
L ying down as they sleep while they cackle and wake them up
O ver and over
W hizzing around the devils go
E vil witches making a spell
E vil devils scaring people
N ow Hallowe'en is over, night-night!

Amber Walsh (11)
Haven High Technology College, Boston

Hallowe'en

H orrid witches,
A nd bats too!
L ove to see me and you,
L ike everyone, especially girls!
O ne person in every world,
W izards and spells all over the place!
E verywhere and everyone,
E specially you in your life!
N ow beware the monster with a knife!

Lauren Limb (11)
Haven High Technology College, Boston

Crisps!

Crisps,
Wonderful crisps,
I eat them every day,
Cheese and onion crisps,
Are so lovely,
So are salt and vinegar,
They are great!

Toni Pragnall (11)
Haven High Technology College, Boston

Witch

W icked witches
  I n the night
  T hey might bite
  C auldrons here, cauldrons there
  H aving their midnight snack.

Cally Bagley (11)
Haven High Technology College, Boston

All About Me

P aige is my name
A nd I have lots of attitude
 I love to go running
G oals are my thing
E ating lots of chocolate and fizzy sweets.

Paige Dunworth (12)
Haven High Technology College, Boston

Sharon

There once was a lady called Sharon,
Who spent all her days in the tavern,
She was offered a job
And gave out a sob,
That lucky lady called Sharon.

Liam Green (12)
Haven High Technology College, Boston

A Silly Young Girl From Paris

There was once a girl from Paris
Who dreamed she lived in a palace
Her mummy the poker
Her daddy the joker
That silly young girl from Paris.

Kirsty Simons (12)
Haven High Technology College, Boston

- The East & West Midlands

The Ghost Cat

Pussy playing with a cotton ball
Hisses at someone in the hall
She screams and yells and gives a shout
So pussy thinks, *I'll go walk-about*

The phone rings, the woman thinks
This silly situation stinks
My wretched cat, how dare she go
Was that car wheels I heard, *oh, no!*

The pussycat was squashed quite flat
And that was just the end of that
She cried and cried and went to bed
And then she bought a dog instead

The woman, she jumped up and down
I got myself a lovely hound
Suddenly, a ghost appeared
An eerie howling could be heard

Oh, no! It's *pussy!* It's our dead cat
I've never noticed she was so fat
'I'm not fat!' the ghost cat said
Hovering slowly above the dog's head

The dog jumped up and took a bite
There was nothing there, which gave him a fright
The dog ran off and ran away
And the ghost cat haunts them every day.

William Hartley (12)
Highfields School, Matlock

Autumn

A utumn is a beautiful time of the year
U nusual colours
T rees are bare, where are the leaves?
U p in the trees sit just the birds
M any leaves on the floor, in the trees . . .
N one!

Chloe Wragg (11)
Highfields School, Matlock

Humans

I think humans are rather mean,
They bully me if I'm seen,
They are huge compared to me,
So little am I to thee.

I think humans are rather mean,
Their feet so big,
They shriek so high,
They want me to die.

I am a mouse,
Some think I'm cute,
Some love me to be seen,
But I think humans are mean.

Leigh Hays (11)
Highfields School, Matlock

The Feeling Of Life

The sound of angels, gentle sounds of angels
Softly singing in your ears
The cold shallow feeling when loved ones cannot be with you
The person you think is a hero is the bad guy
The end of the being and the power of moving on
The feeling of life flashing before your eyes
The things you expect to be untrue are right in front of you
The feeling of trying to push to the next level
The feeling of life, the feeling of death
The feeling of hope, the feeling of happiness
Sometimes life is good, sometimes life is bad
Keep holding on and sad times will no longer be sad.

Michaela Oldfield (12)
Highfields School, Matlock

The Humans

Humans are nice but some are not,
It all depends which one you've got,
Some are kind and like to please,
They will give you bits of cheese,
Some are thin and some are fat,
But the nasty ones they buy a cat,
Humans are big, but some are bigger,
But what scares me is their cat, Tigger,
I don't care if they are big or small,
Because I'm nice and cosy in their wall!

Emily Smith (11)
Highfields School, Matlock

My Wish

My name is Hayley
I would like my own pony
To ride on the ground that's even or stony
I'd groom its coat and make sure it's fed
Then last thing at night, I'd put it to bed
We'd go for a ride, we'd go for miles
Jumping over walls and going through stiles
Now I've told you my story and it isn't phoney
My name is Hayley and I want my own pony.

Hayley Smith (11)
Highfields School, Matlock

Autumn Leaves Haiku

Autumn leaves falling,
Onto the glistening ground,
Twirling as they go.

Charlie Henderson-Howat (11)
Highfields School, Matlock

Me, Little Girl With Trouble

My name is Saghar
I am but eleven

My eyes are swollen
I cannot see

I must be stupid
I must be bad

What else could have made
My daddy so mad?

I wish I were better
I wish I weren't ugly

Then maybe my mommy
Would still want to hug me . . .

I can't speak at all
I can't do a wrong

Or else I'm locked up
All the day long

When I'm awake, I'm all alone
The house is dark

My folks aren't home
When my mommy does come

I try and be nice
So maybe I'll get just

One whipping tonight
Don't make a sound!

I just heard a car
My daddy is back

I hear him curse
My name he calls

I press myself
Against the wall

I try and hide
From his evil eyes

I'm so afraid now
I'm starting to cry

He finds me weeping
He shouts ugly words

He says it's my fault
That he suffers at work

He slaps me and hits me
And yells at me more

I finally get free
And I run for the door . . .

He's already locked it
And I start to bawl.

Saghar Abdolseyed (11)
Hillcrest School, Birmingham

My Mother

Mothers, mothers, are always there,
Mothers, mothers, always care.
Whenever I'm hurt,
Or made a mess of dirt,
My mother is always there to clean it.

Mothers, mothers, are always there,
Mothers, mothers, always care.
She's always there for me,
I know that I can rely on her
And she can rely on me, equally.

Yes, I love you, Mother,
So I definitely don't need any other!

Esraa Rofaydaa Mohamed (14)
Hillcrest School, Birmingham

Inside Me!

I still feel your touch,
When you're not around,
I still hear your voice,
In silence and there's no sound.

You are my strength,
That holds me in pain,
You are my shelter,
That protects me from the rain.

You are the curtain,
That opens with light,
You are the moon and stars,
That brighten up the sky at night.

You are the flower,
That blossoms in the spring,
You are the music,
That gets the party in full swing.

The air goes from my lungs,
When you take my breath away,
You put me back on track,
When my path goes astray.

You are the channel,
That changes over time,
You are the harness that holds
Me on the mountains that I climb.

You are the picture that
I sometimes go inside,
You are the wardrobe,
Where I get scared and hide.

You are the one
That's always there to see,
You're always there around,
'Cause Grandma, you're a part of me.

Aniqah Silvera (13)
Hillcrest School, Birmingham

Dead End

I feel his eyes looking at me
I can't see where he is
I'm walking at night
All alone as I walk down that long, never-ending road
I start to feel my heart racing
Beating out of my chest
I see a shadow in the trees
I walk a little faster
I'm small and young
Scared and observant
All my senses working better than ever
I notice a shadow next to me
It's not mine
I feel his eyes stripping me
I feel one tear run down my cheek
He grabs me
I scream!

The next day
Police come to my house
My home
And say to my mother, father and family . . .
She cries, my father hugs her with tears in his eyes
They walk into my room to see a bed that hasn't been slept in
Mother can't stop crying, as she looks around my room
As they get into the police car
Drive to the police station
I walk with them into a room with a glass wall
There is a bag on the table
I can't hear my mother's cry, probably for the best
Then I see me
Me on the table
Me in the bag.

Emily Baker (13)
Hillcrest School, Birmingham

The Consequence

People thought she was part of the smugs,
Even though most of them deal drugs,
She was one of the five girls in the neighbourhood
And believe me, that isn't something very good,
Every corner of the street she turns,
There is something she needs to learn,
The fact that people are watching her
And if she isn't careful, something surprising may occur.

Her parents say her friends are an influence,
That they're the ones that turned her into a nuisance,
The ones that caused her to join the gang,
Just by talking and a snap of a hand,
People might think she's tough
And indeed, extremely rough,
But deep down inside,
There is something she has been trying to hide,
The fact that she is a coward
And someone who is being over-powered.

People think just because she is part of the smugs, she is cool,
Surely whoever thinks that is a fool,
Because she is forced to deal drugs,
Bu the mean leader of the smugs,
Her life is in great danger,
Caused by a total stranger,
If she had just listened to her mom and dad,
None of this would have turned out this bad,
To the extent of her losing her life,
She didn't even reach the age to be someone's wife,
Life is something you don't have to earn,
But something that shouldn't be wasted and that she had yet to learn.

The moral is - don't waste your life!

Matilda Sandi (11)
Hillcrest School, Birmingham

Noughts And Crosses

All of this confusion,
All of this racism,
Being called a nought or a cross,
It's just so mean, why can't it stop?
Why can't we all be as one?
Not being called a nought or a cross!

Sephy, Callum, anyone in this world,
Separating us humans is so absurd!
Some won't listen to a single word,
Because what some have is called true love,
Why can't we all be as one?
Not being called a nought or a cross!

Pushing, shoving, it's going to be the same for us noughts,
They don't give a damn about what's on our thoughts,
They don't care, they'll do all sorts,
To make sure the world's free of noughts!
Why can't we all be as one?
Not being called a nought or a cross!

Wherever we go, it's just so bad,
In this crazy world we live in,
It's just so sad!
We are all people and humans,
So why do people makes such silly rumours?
Why can't we all be as one?
Not being called a nought or a cross!

Noughts, crosses,
Crosses, noughts,
It's always going to be like this,
Just until someone steps up,
Then maybe they would shut up!

Mariam Jan (13)
Hillcrest School, Birmingham

The Other Side Of The World

The world seems so empty to me
My heart sings depressingly
Like life has come to a sudden halt
Tears come as I solemnly wrote

So what if we don't look the same
So what if we've got different names
I know that I'm black and you're white
But between us we share a bright light

Noughts and crosses, not that much difference
Then why the hard feelings? Why the offence?
Please stop racism, I request
It's just the skin colour that differs from the rest

Then why the continuous fighting
I wonder why they keep on shouting
Why are they calling noughts horrible names?
Haven't they at all any shame?

God has created us all
Though now He must be appalled
The state that we are in
We are committing a big sin

Now's the time we can give respect
Now's the time we can make up for the wrecked
If we all try together to repair
We can mend the special bond that we share

You'll be able to see
Just how much you mean to me
You'll be able to see how things will be twirled
You'll be able to see the other side of the world.

Sonal Patel (13)
Hillcrest School, Birmingham

War

I tell myself,
Be brave,
Chest out,
Chin up,

I try and block the noise around me,
It's hard,
Gunning and bombing,
Screaming and shouting,
From left and right,

My heart,
It's racing,
I'm sweating,
From fear,
Not from the heat of bombs,
My palms are damp,

I've got to do it,
I see an image in my head,
Mother weeping,
Father pacing,
Never knowing if they'll see me again,

I scream,
I've got to do it,
The door's thrust open,
I run,
As fast as I can,
I feel the floor beneath my feet,

Into the deep sadness of war!

Hope Fields (12)
Hillcrest School, Birmingham

My Best Friend, Kemiica

Talk, talk, talk, Kemiica likes talk
People like to show off
People like to hate
People like to fight
People like to kill
People like to swear
People like to moan
People like to shout
Her mum is a tyrant
When I'm relaxing
She hears the loud voice
It's my mum shouting my name
Kemiica
Can you get me a drink?
Can you wash up?
Can you tidy up?
Can you clean the cat's litter?
She didn't want to go to the dinner
At her mum's friends
She wanted to go to a party with her
Friends
The dinner was boring
There were not a lot of children there
Just a five-year-old and a baby
And that was not fair
I should have gone to the party
Yes, Kemiica likes to talk
But for all her talking
I never want to tell her to shut up.

Tamelia Harris (14)
Hillcrest School, Birmingham

Dear Mr Weeping Willow Tree

Dear Mr Weeping Willow Tree

I noticed the way you dance and sway
On a warm summer's eve
When all the kids like to play
In-between your weepingness.

In the winter, you're full of snow
A great event, all the children come
In the winter, a soft wind does blow
But soon the snow melts and once more we see your weepingness

In the spring the water's at it best
On boat going downstream
Before we go home to rest
We must go through your weepiness

In the autumn you stand out from the crowd
As all the rest start to go bald
You stand in the middle tall and proud
You're still green in your weepingness

One day he tried and a good attempt he made
As he climbed up you and your best branch broke
We then realised too late that you couldn't be saved
You were old and dying, no more playing in your weepingness

Now forty years later we were not wrong
Brown and wrinkly as you are
You are not as strong
But even now, I still play in your weepingness.

Charlotte Smith (13)
Hillcrest School, Birmingham

Dumped

She was part of a beautiful life
But it got ruined when she was a wife
To a total stranger
But he was a lot of danger
He was good looking
But that's not what her heart was hooking
When she was 25 they got married
But it was not gonna get carried
By his heart

When she had her first child
She wasn't very mild
She took a lot of drugs
Followed by mugs
She didn't know what she did
But she put herself into prison

When she was out
She didn't know
That he was planning
Something that had a lot of meaning
He had dumped her, like you dump rubbish.

Then she realised that her child was missing
She didn't have a chance to do her kissing
She knew that life is not easy to live
And she didn't have enough love to give
She was part of a beautiful life
That got ruined when she was a wife.

Hibaq Mohamed (11)
Hillcrest School, Birmingham

Feeling Blue

I feel blue sometimes
And I know you feel blue too
Everybody feels blue from time to time
And I know feeling blue isn't a crime
Sometimes you need to feel blue to find the dime inside you.

Mahdi Rahman (11)
Hillcrest School, Birmingham

Time

*Tick-tock, tick-tock,
Round and round the hands on the clock
One minute, two minutes, five, then ten.*

I wake in the morning with the sound of my clock
Buzzing like an aircraft waiting to take off
Oh! I moan, it's time to get up
My eyes are still sticky, my mouth's filled with slime
My mum shouts, 'It's time, it's time!'
I am all ready, I hiss with fear
Hoping my mother didn't hear

I just went to sleep and it's morning already
Time to make the bed
Time to get washed
Time to have my breakfast and medicine too
Time to get dressed and brush my teeth
Time to get my stuff and get ready to leave

I've had a full day at school now and the bell has gone
Chitter-chatter and a whole heap of noise from all the girls
Heading to the cloakroom and rushing through the door
Some live near and some live far
Some travel by foot or in a car
We bid our farewells and go our separate ways
But we all have one thing in common and that is *time*

So, time is important and it should not be taken for granted
So have time, make time and be on time!

Shohanna Nashay Newman Kidd (11)
Hillcrest School, Birmingham

Untitled

We live in a life where hope is the only thing you can do
We hope that one day someone will love us for who we are

We hope that one day we will believe in ourselves
It's time to stop hoping and start doing something
About what we want in life.

Melissa Louise Albutt (15)
Hillcrest School, Birmingham

Lost With Sadness . . .

All hope is gone
I'm surrounded with fear
My heart filled with sorrow
As I let out a tear
I'm drifting away
When I hear all the
Bombs and explosions
My feelings are hurt
As I fill with emotions
Trying to forget
What happened before
I cry in pain, but
What am I really fighting for?
No one there beside me
No one to hear my pain
I don't even have
Something to gain
Because everything is gone
Look what's happened
And what's been done
No family, no friends, no nothing
I've lost it forever
As my last tear drips
I give out a cry
And close my eyes
Hoping I'll die . . .

Abeera Ali (12)
Hillcrest School, Birmingham

Colours Of The World Unite

Pink, purple, black or white
Colours of the world unite
We are all special in our own way
And sometimes there's a price to pay
Green, orange, yellow or blue, I promise
That I'll stand by you.

Billy-Jean McDonnell (14)
Hillcrest School, Birmingham

Friendship Poem!

Friendship is well needed
So that you can tell everyone what we did,
Sometimes people may not be your friend,
This means your friendship has come to an end,
Everyone needs a friend to depend on
Even you need at least one,
When you've got no friends, you're upset,
Maybe the thing to cheer you up is a pet,
You need people to talk to,
The advantage is you can choose who,
In your life you'll need advice,
Make sure you choose someone nice,
A friend is someone you can rely on,
You can't always go to your mom,
Your mom's got things to do
Just like you should do,
Kids should go to the park and play on swings,
Listen to music
And do your own thing,
Choosing a friend is complicated,
Pick the wrong person, you'll think, *I should have waited,*
With friends you play different things,
At the end, compare who wins,
Friends are what you need
In life to succeed!

Sharna Hazell (11)
Hillcrest School, Birmingham

Love

You can fall from the sky,
You can fall from a tree,
But the best place to fall
Is in love with me,
Please listen to what
I have to say,
Because I love you in every way.

Larissa Shaw (14)
Hillcrest School, Birmingham

Off We Go!

3pm packing my bags, being told to leave the country
Sadly leaving my friends
No more playing around
This is when friendship ends
Sitting sadly on my comfy bed, weeping and weeping
My heart is broken
I want to hide
I feel mistaken
Different people to meet and new places to go
Sitting down, remembering
All the memories
How hard it is to let go

4pm sending a note to all those I will miss
It says:
To all you dear friends
I have to leave
I will miss you all
But now I have to find
Someone else who can pick
Me up when I fall
Goodbye my friends

6pm time to go
Time to take memories with me.

Silvia Cheza (13)
Hillcrest School, Birmingham

Sun

Sun, sun so lovely and bright
It's even hot, it's the dark, dull night
Loads of kids going to bed
Thousands of children wiping their head.

Sun, sun so lovely and hot
Mmm! Mmm! Oops! I forgot
Loads of people going to play
It has been a hot, sunny day.

Sherene Lian O'Saye (12)
Hillcrest School, Birmingham

I Am

Do you think I am me because of my colour?
Do you think I am me because of my hair?
Do you think I am me because of my background?
Do you think I am me because of where I live or where I am from?
What I give or what I have done?
What I'll say or what I'll do?
Which path I choose to walk through?
You might be right
But I am not just the girl you see in the street
With the blue and black spotted glasses
I am the girl who listens and gets most things right in her classes
I am not the girl to be seen with the crowd
I get good grades and I'm not that loud
I am not the same as anyone else
I am different, not cloned, I'm unique
I'm not the type to be skipping school
I'll be there all through the week
I am not the girl that messes about and is blank when it comes to a test
I know that by paying attention, I'll always be doing my best
You don't know a lot about who I am
But you know plenty about who I'm not
If ever you are looking for me anywhere
Don't look through the normal lot.

Aalyah Malcolm (12)
Hillcrest School, Birmingham

Untitled

My mum, she is a hard-working woman
She always works from morning to night
She wakes up in the morning
She gets everyone out of bed
She makes my breakfast
She gets me ready for school
All day long she works
Cleaning, cooking, ironing clothes
One day, I want to be like my mum.

Yanci Vangua (15)
Hillcrest School, Birmingham

Weather

Rain, rain
Falling on the street,
Water in socks
Cleaning my feet.

Thunder, thunder
Here it comes,
Close the windows
Keep the doors shut.

Clouds, clouds
Dull and grey,
Heavy with misery
To drop all day.

Sun, sun
Breaking dawn,
Here it comes
The rain stops too.

Rainbow, rainbow
Brightening the sky,
Look at the colours
To brighten my eyes.

Sathvir Kaur (11)
Hillcrest School, Birmingham

Ruby Tanya

(Based on 'Ruby Tanya' by Robert Swindells)

A sad life with fake emotion has no worth living story,
She went to who she calls a father,
Someone who beats her, but for love,
A wealthy man who cherishes his country,
But all he does is shove,
For those who are innocent and are entitled to their own opinion,
Would dislike him a million,
When your flesh and blood wants you behind bars,
You call yourself a father?

Chadene Skerritt (13)
Hillcrest School, Birmingham

Changes

How did people become like this?
All of the fighting
All of the hurting
It shouldn't be like this

We should all work together
To stop the fighting
To stop the racism
Then we'll all be like one

How did it become like this
With all of the pollution
Which the people have made
It shouldn't be like this

We should all be working together
Stop cutting the trees down
To get less CO_2
Then we'll all be working together as one

If we all stick together
Then people can see
How working together
Can make most people very happy.

Nykola Buttress (13)
Hillcrest School, Birmingham

Different Kinds
(Based on 'Ruby Tanya' by Robert Swindells)

My name is Ruby Tanya and I'm quite nice and small
But when I look at others, I say, 'My gosh, you're so tall!'
I like to play with different races, but my dad won't let me
He always says, 'Play with your own race!'
But now it's time to face and take charge
Enough is enough, this has gone on too long
If it carries on anymore, it may turn out as a song
Black, white, Asian and Chinese, we're all different races
So why can't we get along?

Deborah Smith (12)
Hillcrest School, Birmingham

A Faraway Land

On a plane
Flying far, far away,
Crossing the skies
Through the night and day.

Hubbly, bubbly
Stingity hop!
Hover high, hover low
But now do not stop!

Please don't go up
But go lower and lower,
I'm feeling sick
So please go slower!

'We're nearly there,'
My mummy said,
'Nearly in Asia
Then off to bed!'

That was the past
Written in the present,
Next is the future
When the moon is crescent . . .

Razan Adi (12)
Hillcrest School, Birmingham

My Only Choice

I was all alone
And a tear rolled down my cheek
As I saw my parents away
In the distance
I widened my eyes
To reach the sky, up high

But the easiest way
Was to lay down
To die . . .
. . . Restfully.

Sameera Ali (12)
Hillcrest School, Birmingham

Racism

He sits in a dark corner, out of the way,
Thinking about all the hurtful things they say,
He wants to say something back,
But he's scared they might give him a whack,
It's all about the colour of his skin,
But it's a battle he knows he will never win,
He sits at home getting vexed,
Wondering what they'll do next,
His mum can never ask why,
For he's always upstairs having a cry,
To them, he's nothing because of the way he looks,
As they look down on him, he sticks his head in a book,
Hoping one day he can do it
And finally stand against it,
He'll become something one day
And he'll forget about the dreary, grey days,
But there's one thing he should never forget -
It doesn't matter about what race you are,
Or where you come from,
It will always depend on what's inside
And where your heart will lie.

Maina Sandi (11)
Hillcrest School, Birmingham

The Dare

'Dare - wear your uniform backwards tomorrow!'
I didn't know I would be in sorrow
Mrs Air was shout-shout here
And shout-shout there.
It was shouting I couldn't bear,
She called Mom and Dad,
They both went mad.
My excuse was, 'It was Bill,'
Who I couldn't wait to kill!
My mom gave me a good shake,
Now I've learnt by my mistake.

Hirra Chohan (12)
Hillcrest School, Birmingham

Holiday Time

We were going on holiday,
Hip, hip hooray!
It was a chance to get away,
On that awful summer's day.
We were off to Africa the best place to go,
But where was my best teddy bear, Little Po?
I kept searching high and low,
Running back and forwards, to and fro.
It was time to leave,
I begged, oh, please,
I needed a new Po to hug and squeeze.
This wish I received and so we left the house
And very strangely, so did the mouse,
As we scurried along to the airport,
I saw an old man who started to snort!
As we were high in the sky,
I saw a bumblebee flying by.
Once we arrived,
I felt so alive
And now it's time to say goodbye!
Bye!

Sara Ahmed (11)
Hillcrest School, Birmingham

Violation

Why do men violate little girls?
Is it because they have no life?
Or they had it done to them when they were young?
They should not go to prison
And get ten years or so,
They should be punished liked they did in the olden days
So they would really know
What they did has changed lives
Scarred them till their dying days,
No matter what these men do,
These happenings will still come back to haunt you.

Lauren Emma Dyson (14)
Hillcrest School, Birmingham

Summer Holiday

I like holidays
Because we get to see lots
Of new and exciting things.
One summer
I see a poster on the wall,
One week in Turkey,
With flight and hotel,
What great value!
I take the poster
To show my mum.
I say, 'Please, please, please . . .'
She says, 'OK.'

In the aeroplane
I wonder
What will Turkey be like?
What will Istanbul be like?

Every night the cruise ship had parties
With music and dancing
And eating
All at sea.

Kimiya Farjadifar (12)
Hillcrest School, Birmingham

Life In A Grave . . .

My life in a cave,
But one day I will be lying in my grave,
Under mud and I will say,
Let me out, I've been suffering for days,
No one will reply and I will cry,
This is reality, it isn't a lie,
Everyone will have to say their goodbyes.

I'll scream and moan
One thousand groan
I'll cry and weep
With not a moment's peace!

Rumesha Baig (11)
Hillcrest School, Birmingham

Learning Is The Key

Learning is the key, no matter how hard it may be
It can inspire you to get on with it
So that you will grow up to be what you really want to be
It may be hard and boring, happy or sad
But when you get your A level results
And it appears to be good news
You may find your parents are glad
Don't try to hide, it's a good opportunity
For all you know, it is all over the community
Don't ever hide the fact that learning and education
Are things you can sometimes lack
There are many good things to come in the future
Education for one, but the rest
You decide yourself
So remember, learning is the key
No matter how hard it may be
And if you succeed
Then you will really grow up to be
What you really want to be.

Tameka Hemans (12)
Hillcrest School, Birmingham

Fear

Why do we have fear?
Why do we have to be frightened?
Why is this world so scary?

Some people fear dark alleyways
Some people fear spiders
Some people fear walking alone in the dark

I fear spiders as they come close
I fear walking in the dark when I am alone
I fear lots of things in this world, that there are too many to name

Fear is the scariest thing in the world
Fear is all around us
And we have to live with it.

Crystal King (14)
Hillcrest School, Birmingham

Friends Are . . .

Friends are like buttons
All holding a piece of you together

Friends are like guardians
Always got your back

Friends are like editors
Reading you like a book

Friends are like mirrors
Reflecting your emotions

Friends are like cheerleaders
Egging you on

Friends are like the sun
Brightening up your day

Friends are like diamonds
Hard to find and rare

But false friends are autumn leaves
Falling everywhere.

Alisha Aggrey (12)
Hillcrest School, Birmingham

Swifting Sounds

La, la, la
Sing a little song
Have fun all day long!

Hum, hum, hum
Ding, dang, dong
There go the little chimes!

Ting, tang, tong
Play the piano
Have a little fun!

Huff, puff, toot, toot!
As you
Blow into a flute!

Hillery Phillip (11)
Hillcrest School, Birmingham

A Starving Child

This child is starving
There's no food to eat
She cries all day
She cries all night
You can see her bones
Sticking out
You can see her eyes
Full of tears
She begs for money
She begs for food
She doesn't like this pain
She doesn't like the game
Life is so bad
Maybe death is better
This child is starving
There's no food to eat
She cries all day
She cries all night.

Zohal Marofi (13)
Hillcrest School, Birmingham

Music

Music is so cool
If you put it up, it will be loud
I listen to it while playing pool
Lots of people like the sound.

Music is so cool
I listen to it every day
Really they don't fool
So, so cool.

Music is so cool
You must be mad not to like it
Music is so cool
99% of people like music.

Music is cool!

Naila Khan (11)
Hillcrest School, Birmingham

Friendship

Friends are the best thing in the world
Friends are always there for each other
Friends are really close to each other
Friends are never apart wherever they are

Some friends are closer than others
Some friends are friends forever
Some friends are funny
Some friends are serious

My friends are the best
My friends are better than the rest
Wherever they are we are never apart
We will always be best friends forever

Your friends
My friends
Whoever they are
All you need to know is that they will always be there for you.

Lucy Need (14)
Hillcrest School, Birmingham

A Smile Is A . . .

A smile is a sign of love
A smile is a sign of care
A smile is a sign of peace
A smile is a sign of happiness
A smile tells people how much you mean to them
A smile is a sign of hope
A smile is a sign of trust
A smile is the sun in the sky when you're lying on the beach
A smile takes the pain away
A smile makes you happy again
A smile is the wind in your hair
A smile is everything around you
Everyone smiles when they're happy
So don't hide your smile
Smile and let the world know you're happy.

Tamara Albutt (14)
Hillcrest School, Birmingham

Fruit

Oranges are orange
Pears are green
Bananas are yellow
And fruit you have never seen

Grapes are nice
Apples are sour
Mangos are sweet
That you just love to eat

Fruit that are long
Fruit that are small
Fruit that are a ball
Yum, don't you want to eat them all?

Fruit is healthy
It's one of your five-a-day
Maybe if you eat loads of apples
It will keep the dentist away?

Rhiannah Elaine Blake (12)
Hillcrest School, Birmingham

Learning

Learning is an important thing,
You'll never know what it will bring,
There's English, maths and history
Learning is a mystery.

Learning is great, there is no doubt,
Easy and hard, that's what it's all about,
Sometimes there's a pass and sometimes fail,
But you'll certainly know when you've hit the nail.

We sit our tests, brave and bold,
Knowing nothing of what it will hold,
But finally we finish that part,
Even though it's still a worry in our hearts,
So now you know, learning is done everywhere,
Not just a simple here and there.

Amandeep Kaur Behal (13)
Hillcrest School, Birmingham

Black Or White?

What colour is the best?
Because they are all the same,
The only purpose they have,
Is to have someone to blame.

Just because you are black,
They think of you as bad,
They look at you with weird faces,
Just because you are in a place where there are no different races.

Just because you are white,
They think everything you say is lies,
They look, point and make up lies,
Just because you are white.

Black or white?
What colour is the best?
The only purpose they have,
Is to have someone to blame.

Marian Toko Zolana (13)
Hillcrest School, Birmingham

I Believe In You, Mother

I believe in you
When I open my eyes
I believe in you
When I look up into the sky
I believe in you
Because you are everywhere
I believe in you
Because you have always been there.

I would give her all my life
Just to make her live longer
I would give her my strength
To make her stronger.

I love my mummy
She makes me foods that are scrummy.

Lavin Mahmoud (14)
Hillcrest School, Birmingham

Past Memories

Past has gone, it comforts my life,
Someday I wish for it to begin again.
There it is on the table, the knife,
That is going to end my life.

I usually sit on the sofa, staring at the eye,
Beginning to wonder what it is,
Past begins to fade, the noise gets louder,
There I begin, I know it is my brother.

When the dawn comes, I hide my fear,
Of my old naughty, naughty brother,
The terrible noises which I hear,
There are the tears in my mother.

Time goes past and curses happen to be,
Which haunt us all now,
There it is and what we all see,
It all was a show and we all begin to bow.

Arusa Mahmood & Bukky Ajayi (11)
Hillcrest School, Birmingham

Petrified

Petrified is the word that sums it all up
The screeches, the shouts and the screams
The roof collapsing above my head
Twisting the world around me
The throbbing and pounding of my heart
Unexplainable experiences surround me
The uncertainties and fears that lie ahead
Sends a shiver through my spine and mind
Suffering throughout the whole way
Like Hell has befallen us
Unexpectedly landing on the wrong side
Like an accident was meant to happen
What has happened for this day to come
And why is it so dreadfully excruciating?

Aisha Amhar (13)
Hillcrest School, Birmingham

Lies Of Selfishness

All I can hear are bombs and cries
Due to the selfishness and all the lies
Now I am an asylum seeker
It doesn't feel that pleasant
Why can't everyone respect each other and hold hands
No matter what colour?
I go to a different country
Accused of a bombing, I am sent back to torture
Which is where I came from
My dad has been murdered, my mum is being taken to the police station
Now I am an orphan, all lonely and scared
Nobody wants me, because of my nationality
We all have to suffer for everybody else's actions
Why can't they see? All we want is peace!
My mum will always stay in my heart
My family was always there for me
Who will take me now?

Tanzeela Bi Hussain (12)
Hillcrest School, Birmingham

Heart Breaking

Your heart is breaking
And so is mine
But you've just got to look at time
It's easy to say, but don't make love pass you by
Once it has gone, it may never come back
And you will be sitting, wondering where the time went
Remembering the good time we spent together
Crying and hurting, I wish I could go back
Why did you do this to me?
I don't think we deserved to have this heartbreak
We feel it the most at the end of the day
When we are alone, with no one to hold
Why is our heart breaking?

Shantella Palmer (14)
Hillcrest School, Birmingham

Noughts And Crosses

Noughts and crosses
Black and white
What's the difference, please don't fight
It's just a colour, nothing less
It's just a colour, don't be obsessed
My best friend's white, yeah and what?
This boy is special, he means a lot
Him and me, me and him
Walking down the bright, white beach
No! No! Not anymore, discrimination gained control
I wish everything could just be the same
I remember the days when he called my name
I hope this is just a silly game and that nothing did ever change
Noughts and crosses
Black and white
What's the difference? Please don't fight.

Chayonne Lee-Rondelle (13)
Hillcrest School, Birmingham

Words Of Inspiration

You are the star that lightens up my day
And now that you're gone, I don't know what to say
You were there for me when I needed you
And now that you're gone I don't know what to do
As each day goes by, I feel like I'm going insane
The loss of you is so hard, I can feel the pain
Tell me why you had to die, because all I do now is cry and cry
You made me feel like I could fly
Taking me up so high into the sky
People lie and say that everything is going to be alright
How could it be? When you're not here with me
But now I know you are close by, all I have to do is look up into the sky
The brightest star there will ever be, shining so bright,
so that everyone can see
To me you'll never be gone, because your memory will live on and on
So rest in peace, because you will be missed.

Ahliya Hussain (12)
Hillcrest School, Birmingham

Friends

I have friends that are kind,
But someone I can find,
They also are there for me,
'Cause if I hurt my knee,
Look how lovely they are,
I would love them to be in a jar,
When they are outside,
I will have to decide,
Shall I be their friend anymore?
Or will I stay indoors?
Deciding what to do,
Unfortunately, I had flu,
Oh, no! I can't find them,
It's already 10pm,
I can't really believe it,
The moon is already lit.

Nashwa Bayan (12)
Hillcrest School, Birmingham

Learning

Learning, learning is the key to life,
Without knowledge you can't survive.
Learning, learning is a great source,
With English and maths you have a great force.
Learning, learning is the answer to all,
It can make you feel ten feet tall.
Learning, learning, you think it's uncool,
But when you're clever you're the one who rules.
Learning, learning what you don't know,
It can help your knowledge grow.
Learning, learning is a bore,
But you have to do it by the law.
Learning, learning is a strength,
It may feel like a long length.
Learning, learning is a matter,
Without a brain you would shatter.

Rahma Abdi Osman (13)
Hillcrest School, Birmingham

Friends

Water may dry
Flowers my die
But good friends
Will never say goodbye
They're there for each other
Love one another
Can't help but deny their friendship is no lie
People may try to destroy it
But friends won't obey it
Friends will never forget each other
No matter what
They will enjoy friendship until the last pot
At the end of the day seeing your friend
Will make you say
Hip, hip
Hooray!

Jasmin Gill (11)
Hillcrest School, Birmingham

Me, Myself And I

M e, myself and I!
A lways reaching for the sky!
I nteresting, intelligent, or so I've been told!
M ake a dream and to that I'll hold!
O h, what else can I say?
O verall, I get better by the day!
N aughty I can be!
A ctually, that part you'll never see!
H ighs and lows are part of life, happiness is all I strive!

B eautiful!
A dventurous!
T otally!
O wesome!
O kay, that's a spelling mistake!
L et's just say I'm . . . *me!*

Maimoonah Batool (11)
Hillcrest School, Birmingham

Learning Is A Blessing

Learning is a rhyme,
It takes all of your time.
It can be very hard,
Rather like making a card.
But if you want to succeed,
You have to be the best you can be.

College, uni and school,
Each of them are cool.
A levels, exams and GCSEs,
All that hard work will pay off, you'll see.
As long as you try,
There's no need to cry.

And don't take a strife,
Education is your life.
You may hear it on the TV,
Of what people don't want to be.
But if you think about it your way,
When you sit your exams, everything will be OK
And *remember,* learning is a blessing.

Kaprhys Lee-Bryan (12)
Hillcrest School, Birmingham

Why?

Why? When I look around, a tear comes to my eye,
There's rubbish on the street and pollution in the sky
It's damaging the world can't you see?
Can anyone help me?
Don't you mind the litter on the streets?
Can't you see it not making ends meet?
Do you want your grandchildren to grow up like this,
With pollution in the mist?
Do you want racism to be their spoken language?
So, next time you have a can of Coke,
Put it in the bin and make the world a better place.

Sarah Megan Johnson (13)
Hillcrest School, Birmingham

It Was There!

I saw it, it was there
It was, I swear, I did see it
Do you believe me? It was staring into my eyes
It was, please believe me
Mom, it was there, I did see it
Do you believe me?
It ran into my bedroom, I . . .
Screamed . . . I am not hallucinating . . .
It was there, I saw it
Those big blue eyes were staring at me
I was scared, then I tumbled out
Of *bed,* I got up and then . . .
I did say I was *not* hallucinating.

Princess Bogle (15)
Hillcrest School, Birmingham

O' Mother!

My mother is my everything, my world
And my heart
I always seem to miss her
When we are far apart
No matter how stressful and embarrassing
She can be, I will always know she is
So special to me
Through bad times, through good times
She will always be there to take her responsibilities
And show me she cares
I love my mom, she brought me into this world
And no matter what, I will always be her
Little girl.

Aaliyah Spence (15)
Hillcrest School, Birmingham

Jealousy

I notice everything you do
You're so cool and different
How I'd love to be you
Because I'm alone and distant

I wish upon a star
That my life could change
Looking up in the dark
Every day it rains

I've decided, that I don't wanna ever just be
I've decided, to take a look at the real me
I've decided, that I don't wanna live this way
I've decided, I won't ever walk away.

Luanda Holness (13)
Hillcrest School, Birmingham

Why?

Either black, either white
There's always a great big fight
Sadly some don't think for a moment
That really life is way more important

Still so many people getting judged by their race
For peace we all want, is there such a place?
And racism only leads to sadness and war
Just goes to show how ignorant some are

So really, we should stop the hate
There's no need for such a debate
We all have personalities we're all the same kind
So let's stop this fight and let's all combine.

Divine Maguraushe (13)
Hillcrest School, Birmingham

End Racism Poem

We all must bring our racism to end,
A message to all I long to send,
The colours of the world all join as one,
All cultures we should share.

The eyes of hate stare down upon you,
Prices of pain release the marks upon you,
The paper of hope is torn in half,
Racism, racism, all it does is laugh.

Life is all an informal hitch,
Laying you down in a big, black ditch,
Fighting against it all worlds collide
And all you can do is sit there and cry.

Simran Kaur Chahal (12)
Hillcrest School, Birmingham

ABC

When you learn not to be in a rush,
Life will give you a helpful push,
Never learn too fast, too slow,
You'll be alright, just go with the flow.

Skipping school, getting detentions,
The job you want will give you rejections,
Science, English or geography course,
Do what you want, but not due to force.

The outside world is waiting for you,
So go out there and try something new,
Grades, reports on your CV,
Queen of knowledge, no more TV.

Kamohelo Modipa (12)
Hillcrest School, Birmingham

Learn Success

Learning to dance is my passion,
I am not a girl who just thinks about fashion,
I want to succeed enough to live in a mansion,
But only if I stay in school and avoid a detention.

As the music beats, beat by beat,
It travels down my rhythmic feet,
I have to be good at all of my subjects,
That way my life will lead to be successful and correct.

What's wrong with learning English and art?
You'll end up being very smart!
You should know it's not against the law,
Because learning earns you more and more.

Kiran Singh Sole (12)
Hillcrest School, Birmingham

My Life

My name is Damilola Ola
And I love drinking Cola.
I live in a country called Nigeria
And now I drink Ribena.

I live with people who think they're cool,
But actually they act like big fools.
I've got two brothers; one mother;
Forget the others; it's not a bother.

I live in a mansion,
Which I think is a great attraction.
I love my room,
Which is made from my mum's groom.

Damilola Ola (11)
Hillcrest School, Birmingham

Silent Flowers

Standing on their high-up stems,
Holding up their crowns,
Getting blown around in the wind,
Bobbing up and down.

Colourful petals like little gems,
Going all around,
Showing all the beauty they've got,
Not making a single sound.

Swifting from side to side,
With a bunch of their friends,
Even though one has been destroyed,
Their beautiful nature never ends.

Ammaarah Ali (11)
Hillcrest School, Birmingham

Emotions

(Based on 'Ruby Tanya' by Robert Swindells)

I sit down with my head down,
I used to hear power within my soul,
I sit down with my head down,
With tears falling down,
As my head's spinning round and round,
Figuring what to do,
So I bring my head back up
And think what I can do to cheer up,
With tears falling down with laughter,
My head's down
And now I have a cuddle off my mother and father.

Keanne Bryan-Hakeem (13)
Hillcrest School, Birmingham

Love

Love means a lot to me,
When you feel it, it burns and stings,
It gives you pain,
It breaks into pieces when I think about it,

But when love comes my way,
It makes love sweet as honey.

Without love this world would be hatred,
When loves turns bad, it ruins your life,
Your heart turns cold as white as ice,
It ruins your life,

So remember, love is important!

Sarah Abdoun (12)
Hillcrest School, Birmingham

A Beauty

I think I'm beautiful, so are you,
You might not feel it, but it's true.

Even if you wear glasses or have a tattoo,
Even if you have braces, or not the nicest shoes,
You are beautiful and that's true.

It doesn't matter what your friends say,
Just follow your heart, it will lead you the right way.

Remember this, looks matter, so don't throw them away,
But don't get obsessed and throw your personality down the drain
And always remember I'm beautiful, so are you,
Keep it neutral, keep it cool!

Rene Nembhard (12)
Hillcrest School, Birmingham

Imaani - It's All About Me!

I maani is forgetful and she never listens,
   But when she works hard, she shines so much, she glistens.
M ysteriously, she only hears what she wants to hear,
   Like if she can have a chocolate biscuit or a chocolate bar.
A ccidentally she fell and bumped her head a put a scar there,
   Now when she frowns and looks down, you can see it there.
A lways doing the wrong thing, she gets herself into trouble,
   Like opening her big, fat mouth and giving people attitude.
N ever does she tell the truth (well, not all the time)
   And you can only trust her sometimes.
I ncredible is she (not really) and when she works hard you can see,
   The girl she's supposed to be.

Imaani Mitchell (11)
Hillcrest School, Birmingham

The Learning Of Learning

We truly learn something every minute
To learning there's no limit
We shall call it 'the cycle of learning'
Because the cycle never stops turning
Imagine you were as clever as Shakespeare
You only have to tune into the right gear
The brain is beyond amazing
When it thinks it starts blazing
With learning you don't need a key
The knowledge is padlock free
Some people say they don't know
That's when they stoop too low.

Sahar Saffari (12)
Hillcrest School, Birmingham

Guess My Life

Look at me, what do you see
Me down on my knees
Praying for a better life
Even though we have guns and knives
It's better than fatal diseases
And me pleading
For my child not to die from Malaria and diarrhoea
And here comes Bin Laden, bombing up all the houses
Now I dodge all the creepy crawlies and the woodlice
Oh, great, now what have I got to lose
Even though I've lost everything I ever had and cared for
See now, I don't feel good, I feel suicidal.

Destiny Williams (13)
Hillcrest School, Birmingham

The Victim

He is the victim of racism and discrimination
He is from a different nation
When white meets black at the same time
To everyone you have committed a crime

Creating an atmosphere of hate
Being white and a man in his fate
Discrimination is always on his plate

He is the victim of racism and discrimination
He is from a different nation
When white meets black at the same time
To everyone you have committed a crime.

Aleena Mahmood (13)
Hillcrest School, Birmingham

My Poem

So this poem's meant to be about me
If you don't believe it, carry on reading and then you'll see.
When I was born, my mom called me Mercedes
But now I'm grown-up, she calls me a lady.
I've got a little brother and I'm getting a little sister
And when she is born, I really want to kiss her.
Now I'm coming to the future,
Hopefully this is not so rubbish, I won't need a tutor.

The grass is green, the clouds will stay white
And all the people will still say goodnight.

Goodnight!

Mercedes Cunningham (11)
Hillcrest School, Birmingham

Vegetables, Vegetables

Vegetables, vegetables, on my plate
All different sizes and colours too.

Vegetables, vegetables, cooking in a pot
No wonder why they are so yucky.

Cauliflower, peas, sprouts and carrots
They all are horrible, so what is the point?

Vegetables, vegetables, they make me sick
Why can't we have chips instead.

Vegetables, vegetables, I hate them so much
I'm stuck here right now with veg on my plate.

Roché Campbell (11)
Hillcrest School, Birmingham

Mixed Reactions

I'm a cross, you're a nought,
Fair enough, that's what I thought.
Didn't know a sin that needs to be forgiven,
A difference that I believe in.
Why am I getting mixed reactions?
Why can I feel the friction?
What matters most is if you stay true to yourself,
Who cares about anyone else?
Just be you,
Do what you want to do,
The true, beautiful you.

Catherine Fadashe (14)
Hillcrest School, Birmingham

I Fear

I fear what happens next
Would I suffer in pain, from fighting in rain?
Bombing homes, with banging tones,
Death around is just what I felt,
Punched to the ground with screaming sounds,
Treated like a goat when soldiers halt,
Sadness makes and I start to daze,
But until that day,
Happiness proud, no one to frown,
A smile on my face,
But in the end, I passed away.

Michelle Cheung (12)
Hillcrest School, Birmingham

I Really Love School!

I really love school!
It is very cool
The lessons you learn
Make you want to turn
You don't want to rush
Because you might break your foot
The rhythm you hear
The beat you can take that
If the beat to your learning break
Don't forget to turn
Or you will not learn.

Connie George Alice Hackley (12)
Hillcrest School, Birmingham

Witch

Witch! Witch!
Hear me chant
As I run I start to pant
Roar! Roar!
Give me no more
As they sleep, they start to snore
Hoot! Hoot!
I'm shaking in my boots
I can hear those trains as they toot
Rats, bats and black cats
Eyes staring as I approach my doormat.

Khianne Sherelle Nelson (13)
Hillcrest School, Birmingham

Snakes

Slithering, slithering, slithering snakes,
The hissing sound it usually makes,
Big, tall, long or short,
Don't worry, you'll never be caught!

Black, white, brown or green,
Those are the colours you might have seen,
This is the colour you might find on a snake,
Even the ones who lurk down the lakes!

Don't forget, stay alive,
Never give up and try to survive,
This was the story of slithering snakes
And the hissing sound it usually makes!

Patricia Tamayem (11)
Hillcrest School, Birmingham

Home Happy And Sad!

I was so happy when my mom said
We were going to Florida
I was all excited to go ahead
Months went by, the days went past
Did not know it would go so fast
I didn't want to say goodbye to my friend
Around the end
So now I'm all happy and filled with joy
I've moved in
And I'm in love with Troy.

Alana Campbell (13)
Hillcrest School, Birmingham

The Bear And A Cat

The bear was living in a flat
Then came along a black and brown cat
The cat asked the bear if she could stay
The bear said sure if you have to, get me a jar of sweets every day
Then the bear went to his room to watch the telly
But the cat came in and screamed that the room was very smelly
The cat sprayed the room then put it away
That smells horrid
No it doesn't.

Deneshae Thomas (11)
Hillcrest School, Birmingham

School Wimps

School is for wimps
Wimps go to school
That's what I think
Reading, writing, why should we do it all?
Dresses for boys, what a dork!
Saw a little boy crying for his mummy
Only five, he's still alive
I felt sorry for him - *not!*
What a wimpy child!

Chardaya Daka (12)
Hillcrest School, Birmingham

Black And White

We see the world
Through black and white eyes
Censoring the brightness
Forgetting about the sky

We think all that matters
Is our black and white lives
But just think about the bright world
And the multicoloured sky.

Kamika Ferguson (13)
Hillcrest School, Birmingham

When School Is Out!

When school is out,
You have to watch out,
Because kids are out,
Not looking around.

Children never care about their road safety
All they care about are fun and games
So when the children are out
Drivers, look out!

Jade Loxton (11)
Hillcrest School, Birmingham

Colours Of Emotion

Blue because my heart is as pure as an ocean's waves,
Red because my passion is strong,
Green because my coma's deep,
Yellow for my energetic love for you,
Pink because my love will stand till the end of time,
Orange for the sunset's best,
Navy for my cool winter breeze,
Emotion, because I live for colour.

Seraphina Codner Okundaye (13)
Hillcrest School, Birmingham

Looking For A Sign

Which is correct: love or hate?
That is the phrase up for debate.
Being an asylum seeker looking for love,
Hoping one day I'll get a message from above.
Why is society so mean and cruel?
Why do they make me out to be the fool?
Young ones learning all this hate
Can we save this cruel world or is it too late?

Sian Mills (12)
Hillcrest School, Birmingham

Learning

Learning, learning, what you don't know,
Learning, learning, like playing in the snow.
Learning, learning, across the nation,
Learning, learning, with your creation.
Learning, learning, be the best of your ability,
Learning different things is up to you and me.
Learning helps you to succeed in life,
Learning can even save your life.

Chante Austin (12)
Hillcrest School, Birmingham

Freedom

F is for . . . free, let me be free
R is for . . . real life is real
E is for . . . everyone has the right to be free
E is for . . . everyone in the world counts
D is for . . . don't ever give up your hopes and dreams
O is for . . . one person can live a better life if you try
M is for . . . many people don't have the things you do - *think!*

Rochelle Cranstoun (12)
Hillcrest School, Birmingham

Communities

The world is a family
Treat it like your own
Asian, Chinese, Indian
Somalian and Moroccan
All a part of our community
The human population.

Kirsty Ellikers (12)
Hillcrest School, Birmingham

Animal Cruelty

Grunting and squealing,
The seals only wanted food,
Now look what they're in for!

Hearing them squeal,
From miles away,
How can this be?

In the tropical countries,
The bears are reduced to pets,
Chained up, made to dance!

Not hearing them roar,
Not a sound while in cages,
How can this be?

Deep in the jungle,
They hide in the trees,
Unaware of their fate!

They suddenly see one,
One of their own, carried away,
How can this be?

Animal cruelty,
It happens all the time,
But how do the animals know?

Hayley Cross (12)
King Edward VI Camp Hill School for Girls, Birmingham

Discrimination

Why do we judge people by their looks?
Why don't we judge them by their soul?
Why can't we all be equal?
Why can't we unite as a whole?

Why do we differentiate between boys and girls?
When both are just the same,
Sometimes girls are better than boys,
But the sexism puts them to shame.

Why do we prefer pretty to ugly,
When ugly people might be great?
Everyone's beautiful on the inside,
So everyone should meet the same fate.

Does it really matter if you're black or white?
So why do people care?
Don't abuse people because of their colour,
Their despair is just too unfair.

What do you care what I believe in?
Whether I'm Hindu, Christian or Jew,
I'm entitled to my own beliefs,
It's my religion, my life, my view.

Akanksha Anand (12)
King Edward VI Camp Hill School for Girls, Birmingham

A Girl's Love

The wind is in the trees,
Silence in the air,
A feeling all around,
Of hopelessness and despair.

A dripping breaks the silence,
A tree creaks under weight,
A girl is hurt and lonely,
And full of burning hate.

She sits up in her tree,
Right outside his home,
Tormenting and calling,
Until he gives a moan.

One day he broke her heart,
But it will never heal,
She'll come here every day,
And stare and watch and feel.

She will not let go,
Of what he did to her,
She meant nothing to him,
Only a space filler.

Bethany Evans (13)
King Edward VI Camp Hill School for Girls, Birmingham

Staying Put

I ain't ever moving house.
I've lived here since I was the size of a mouse.
It might not be huge and it hasn't a pool
But if I moved house I'd be a fool.
All the memories and all the fun, the games
I've played with my sisters and mum
In the summer it's cool, in the winter it's warm.
If I moved house I'd be a proper gorm.
It's often noisy and sometimes a mess
But I love my house, I think it's the best.

Elina Bannister (13)
Lees Brook Community Sports College, Derby

Cancer, My Killer

So ridiculous, so tiny,
It started as a small lump,
Then gradually spreading across my hopeless body.

Just one puff,
Just one drag,
That's all it takes.

My determined to survive lungs are fighting for hope.
There's no hope for me now, it's too late.

It's travelling,
Travelling right through me,
I can feel it.
I depart this humankind planet with pain and suffer.
When I'm in paradise,
I'll be at rest.
I will have a never-ending sleep
I will never wake up out of.

Daniel William Buckley (15)
Lees Brook Community Sports College, Derby

Concentration Camp

Old men, young men, little boys at the camp,
All their beds so very damp.
Don't know what they're doing,
Don't know where they're going.
Most of them are all so starving,
Some children burst into tears,
Others go crazy, killing with spears.

They watch their life just waste away,
Others just stay, in their camp stations,
Some men just haven't got the patience.
'You've just got to get on with life,'
That's what they say!
'You only have one life,
So let's live it our way!'

Jodee Leszczyszak (13)
Lees Brook Community Sports College, Derby

Striped Pyjamas

His face pressed against the wire fence
Wondering where they were going
All these people in striped pyjamas
Looking pale, frail, not knowing.

'Father, why are they all in pyjamas
Are they all going to their bed?
They all go into those rooms
Is there nothing can be said?'

God said that all men are equal
So why are we doing this?
Is it a matter of life and death
If your name is on the list?

How can I put on my striped pyjamas
And go to my nice warm bed
Knowing that when I wake up tomorrow
All those people will be dead?

Jordan Brewin (13)
Lees Brook Community Sports College, Derby

Diversity In The Playground

They call across the playground pointing at me
Shouting, 'How ugly is she!'
She hides in a corner, heart beating fast
Thinking how can this cruelty possibly last
No one to love and no one to care
What they are doing is just not fair
She is not different to any other
It's just because of her skin and colour
It's time to fight back and say what's right
And put an end to this big fight
We want people to stop and care
This goes to people everywhere
We can stop racism at last
So we can now put it all in the past.

Lauren Beavis (13)
Lees Brook Community Sports College, Derby

Untitled

My hands tied in chains rubbing against my soft skin.
Blood slowly dripped on the grey, cold stone floor.
Slowly a soldier's hand stretched out and grabbed me by my chains.

He forcefully dragged me across the floor,
My chains scraping against it,
It was like a teacher scraping chalk on a chalk board but worse.
The soldier lifted me and pushed me in the chair.

A great outburst of light hit my eyes like a nail being hammered in my eye.
A mysterious man lifted up my trousers and examined my scars.
Slowly touching them, it felt I was being hit constantly.
The man swayed to the soldier,
I slowly listened and burst into tears.
This time the soldier told me stand up,
Holding a gun behind my back - made me walk to the showers
I did a quick pray, it felt my heart was ripped out then . . .

Gavon Toor (13)
Lees Brook Community Sports College, Derby

Waiting

The broken world is standing still,
While great armies march out to kill.
The lovely landscape is no more,
It stood proud with a smile before.
Now everything is dull and grey,
No children now go out to play.
The streets are silent and neglected,
The entire world has been affected.
No one talks of anything but loss of lives,
Of brothers, sisters, husbands and wives.
Love and happiness are locked away,
It will come back, we hope, one day.
Until then I'm with my friends
And waiting for when the war ends.

Peggy Watkins (12)
Lees Brook Community Sports College, Derby

The War

People that grew up in the war
End up dead on the floor
And everyone else is poor
Knocking on people's doors.

My grandad was in the war
He was such hardcore
And everyone else is poor
Knocking on people's doors.

It started all so bright
Until there was a big fight
And then it fell to night
The war would never end.

Daniel Dabbs (13)
Lees Brook Community Sports College, Derby

The Old House

Moving house was very boring,
But I will get to see my family every morning,
My dad's upstairs,
My mum's downstairs,
The garden is a mess with the lawn up high,
The maid called Mary is very shy.

The rug in the new house has got loads of holes in,
The new fish my dad got me is missing a fin,
People outside are walking,
My brother and sister are talking,
Now I am going to bed,
To rest my weary head.

Jordan Wynne (14)
Lees Brook Community Sports College, Derby

Racism . . .

Is a piece of plastic,
It never rots away,
It only pollutes the environment
And accumulates
Dirt in the world.

Racism is bad,
Stop it,
It makes me so sad,
I cry
And cry every night,
But it's
The one I will fight.

Harvey Redfern (13)
Lees Brook Community Sports College, Derby

The Fox

The fox crept through the field
At the approach of nightfall.
All was silent.

The sun rose and the birds cried.
All lights turned on.
The fox ran back to the forest
Until night fell again.

Back to the usual,
Only it was not so quiet.
The fox had struck.

Rebecca Helm (11)
Lees Brook Community Sports College, Derby

Childhood

Clouds and rainbows were something we believed we could touch.
Ice cream and chocolate were all we wanted to eat.
The older kids were some kind of giants,
But growing up things changed.

School became something we had to work in,
It wasn't just a playground,
Friends were the people you would do anything for,
And were there for you through everything - they were keepers.

Life was great, nothing would ever make us unhappy.

Dina Harrison (13)
Lees Brook Community Sports College, Derby

Friendship Is One And Only!

Friendship is incredible
Nothing could ever beat it
Sometimes there will be fall outs but most of all laughs!
So remember always you're so lucky to have a friend like you do!

Sometimes there's hatred
And sometimes happiness
But if that ever does happen
Just remember to make sure you remember the happy memories
And be friends for evermore!

Sophie Jarman (11)
Lees Brook Community Sports College, Derby

My Best Mate

My best mate Harry,
Is always there,
When I am down he tries to make me laugh.

My best mate Harry,
We always have a laugh,
He always comes over
And we always take care of my bro.

Tye Booker (12)
Lees Brook Community Sports College, Derby

Friendship

Friendship is like no other
The one you want to hold close.
It makes you feel loved and special,
They're the ones you love the most.

Some days you have regrets
But others you just laugh
About those awfully special days.
And I think to myself
I'm so very lucky to have that one special friend.

Rosie Hatton (11)
Lees Brook Community Sports College, Derby

Untitled

People fought in the war,
Dead bodies all over the floor,
People running for their lives,
Stopping and giving each other hi-fives.

A man called Marvin,
Was very starvin',
Using a flame thrower
Or I might use a lawn mower.

Callum Holler (13)
Lees Brook Community Sports College, Derby

Animals

Monkeys swing from tree to tree,
Eating everything they see,
Fruit, lettuce, bananas and nuts,
They'll get fat if they eat too much.

Elephants stomp by,
People watching them go by,
Bigger than a bamboo tree,
I just wish they were smaller than me.

Megan Lambert (11)
Lees Brook Community Sports College, Derby

Childhood

Growing up in life is a hard thing.
Learning to walk and talk,
Make new friends,
But most of it is great,
Like having your first sleepover
And the first time you ride a bike.
First days back at school,
So live life the way you will enjoy it!

Tegan Stacey (14)
Lees Brook Community Sports College, Derby

The War

Everyone hates when the war begins
Because of what trouble it brings.
The streets become bare
And the children don't seem to take much care.
Their parents all start to begin to worry
And they're always in a hurry.
Until the war comes to an end
Then everything starts to mend.

Megan Frost (11)
Lees Brook Community Sports College, Derby

Untitled

Dead bodies on the floor
I just remembered it's the war
All of a sudden there was a knife
Before his eyes was his life
I picked up a gun
Then had some fun
I was in good camo
Then ran out of ammo.

Jordan Makulow (13)
Lees Brook Community Sports College, Derby

Nearing Midnight

When it's nearing midnight,
Everybody gets a sudden fright,
It's like in space,
You can't even do up your shoelace,
Everywhere is still,
When you look over your window sill,
All is silent in the night,
Until you see a horrible sight.

Kelsey Hughes (11)
Lees Brook Community Sports College, Derby

Hungry

I sat around on the ground
Starving and hungry, tummy rumbling
I saw a chicken, finger lickin'
Sitting on the ground
With half a leg looking nice and round
I got a knife, cut a sliver of head and liver
And ate it all for my dinner.

Michael-Thomas Percy (13)
Lees Brook Community Sports College, Derby

My Dog Bella

My dog Bella,
Is a bit of a smeller,
But I don't care,
Because she's always there,
She may not be clever,
But she's the best dog ever!

Georgina Bruce (11)
Lees Brook Community Sports College, Derby

Wildlife Is Everywhere

Wildlife is in the air,
Search high and low, you'll find it there.
Bugs here and bugs there,
Wildlife is everywhere.
Some will crawl and some will fly,
Some will live and some will die.

Lauren Welsh (11)
Lees Brook Community Sports College, Derby

My Friend Fred

My friend Fred
Found a bomb in a shed
The bomb blew up
Lots of shrapnel flying in the air
Fred landed on an old bed
With shrapnel in his head.

Daniel Atkins (11)
Lees Brook Community Sports College, Derby

My Mate Billy

I once had a friend called Billy
Who was very silly
He once went to town
Searching for a pound
To pay for his chilli.

Benjamin Smith (11)
Lees Brook Community Sports College, Derby

Why Do People Cheat?

People cheating, it does my head in
All I would like to do is play a game of footie without those who do,
Even though I still have fun scoring goals till the game is done.
Why do people cheat?

Bradley Paul Steptoe (12)
Manor Park Community School, Nuneaton

Where Are You?

I went to school
No one was there
I went to the playground
No one was there
Everyone was gone . . .

I looked everywhere
Everyone was gone
So I stopped
I walked and walked
Couldn't find anyone.

So I went home
No one was there
I checked at work
No one was there
There was no one to care.

I looked up
Someone was there
He came to care
He looked after me
Until my parents came back.

Melanie Norton (11)
Manor Park Community School, Nuneaton

Lonely Snowman

One cold winter night
A snowman stood on the icy ground
With a hat and scarf
All alone

All he wanted was
For someone to come and hug him
He waited and waited
But still no one came
Eventually he gave up waiting
And in anger he melted away.

Dylan Bloore (11)
Manor Park Community School, Nuneaton

Why?

Why am I different to you?
Tell me, why?
Why do you pick on me?
Tell me, why?
Why can't I play with you?
Tell me, why?
Why am I the game?
Tell me, why?
Why don't you like me?
Tell me, why?
Why do you call me names?
Tell me, why?
Why do you hurt me?
Tell me, why?
Why do you make me feel confused?
Tell me, why?
Why does all this happen to me?
Just tell me, why?

Keeley Michelle Harding (12)
Manor Park Community School, Nuneaton

When I Got Bullied!

When I got bullied I didn't do anything.
When I got bullied I felt sad.
When I got bullied I always lost.
When I got bullied I was hurt.

Then one day I had the guts.
I went to the teacher and told what had happened.
The headteacher told him that one day it would end in tears.
That very day I went home happy.

Now I am happy.
The bullying has stopped.
I will always remember that day.
Me and my bully are friends.
I know now how to deal with that.

Lauren Grantham (11)
Manor Park Community School, Nuneaton

Anorexia

I had always loved food,
It gave me strength and talent,
I'm fat which is ugly,
I know I have great friends that love me,
I know I'm starving my inner child,
But I need to feel beautiful,
It's all I want to be,
I feel weak,
It always hurts,
Every day and every night,
My mum told me we would get through this together,
I thought she broke her promise,
I was in hospital,
She showed me some magazines of fat people,
I realised my mum was right,
Now I'm back, I've got strength,
Thanks Mum, you're the best.

Megan Karsten (11)
Manor Park Community School, Nuneaton

Building Up Courage

Starting a new school can be difficult
But making friends can be even more difficult.
Friends aren't always what they seem to be.
They turn against you.
They laugh at you
And eventually they hit you.
Getting hit by one of your best friends is hard.
It's upsetting.
It makes you feel frightened in case they hit again.
Is there a way to stop it?
Yes, there is.
Build up your courage and tell someone.
That's what I did and it helped me.
My life was happier, I was no longer upset,
I was happy.

Rhys Jones (11)
Manor Park Community School, Nuneaton

It!

Who's got it?
Nobody knows,
Everyone says they've got it!
Not really, they're all just pathetic.
Talking about it.
What is it?
It is a statement
Which everyone tries to have,
But nobody gets it.
So make your jokes,
Go on, I dare you.
At least I can say no I don't have it.
It is something you earn.
And I've earned it.
But I don't want it,
I can live without it.

Carly Jackson (12)
Manor Park Community School, Nuneaton

Things Can Change!

Life can be hard sometimes,
You can get hurt physically and emotionally,
Called names, punched,
I've been through it all,
There's been blood, sweat and tears,
I've been sworn at,
Kicked, hurt and punched,
I felt melancholy,
The worst thing of all is that nothing was done,
But when I got to secondary school,
It all changed,
Things got better . . .
I've been welcomed with open arms,
Made new friends,
So you can see,
Things can change.

Declan Lloyd (11)
Manor Park Community School, Nuneaton

2009 Generation

You hear it on the news and see it in faces,
Of violence and killings,
But who will change it?

With 16 and 17 year-olds being drug addicts,
Young kids into bullying,
Clever kids being dumb,
Children staying out from as young as 4,
Violent killings turning into games,
Writing into graffiti,
Building blocks into vandalism,
Woodwork into arson,
Sweets into drugs,
Juice into alcohol,
Whatever next? When will it change,
When we join together.

Andrew Barton (11)
Manor Park Community School, Nuneaton

My Grandma

My grandma is many things, but there is *always* one thing
That makes me want to scream!

When I was round and I found some new friends
They were on a fashion trend. When they saw my grandma
It made me want to *flee!* Oh Grandma, *why* embarrass me?

When my cousins were there
I was too, it was a scare!
To find my embarrassing grandma
Was yelling at my grandad!
Then to find out, that made me want to *shout*,
'Oh Grandma, *why* hog?'
Oh no, it was over the dog!
My grandma was something but just to find
She was just trying to be loving, sweet and kind!

Siannon Garrett (11)
Manor Park Community School, Nuneaton

Power

I have a power
A power to win
I have a power
A power to be me
I have a power
A power to stand up for my people
I have a power
A power to do as I will
I have a power
A power to look like what I want

My power is my own
We all are unique
I am me and nobody can change me.

Keira Jones (12)
Manor Park Community School, Nuneaton

Bad Failure

There was a girl who was so young
Who got bullied for her one lung,
Even though she couldn't fight back
She still had bruises that turned black.
Her mum had tried to make it better
So to cover her scars she had a sweater.
She never thanked her mum for that
Because at school she was the local bat.
She then met a girl who stopped
Her head getting swirled and twirled.
So now she's fit and ready for action
But she never wants to go back
To that distraction ever again.

Nicole Louise Jacques (11)
Manor Park Community School, Nuneaton

Love Is Something That . . .

Love is something that makes you smile,
Love is something that makes you sad.
Love is something that makes you happy,
Love is something that makes you cry.

Love is something that makes you strong,
Love is something that makes you scared.
Love is something that makes you wonder,
Love is something that helps you find.

Love is something that is sometimes right,
Love is something that is sometimes wrong.
Love is something that makes friendship,
Love is something that breaks friendship.

Sorrel Sutton (12)
Manor Park Community School, Nuneaton

School

The school began, lots of children go to school
For learning some things and to be clever.
School is a fun part in your life and happiness.
In school you could do anything
Such as have some experiments in science lab.
You can also enjoy playing different kinds of sports.
You can also learn information of different stuff.
In the school you are also capable of making friends
With foreign countries' people like India, Nepal etc.

Hope you like school very much!
When you close your eyes and realise it
You will feel reborn to a child when you go to school!

Anil Gurung (12)
Manor Park Community School, Nuneaton

Bullying

People being bullies
Are always immature
But they never think about the girl next door
They think she's spoiled
But maybe she's not
They always ride round and round the block
People say she's evil
Because she's quiet
And never starts a riot
But just maybe if people gave her a chance
They would see the real her
And let a light shine bright.

Jade Hildreth (12)
Manor Park Community School, Nuneaton

Depression

Depression is very sad,
It makes me feel very bad.
Makes me happy because I need to be happy,
Because depression is not cool.

I want to be happy,
I want to be happy now because
I don't want to be depressed for my time now.

I don't want to be sad
I want to be happy
So turn around and don't be so chatty
Don't be depressed because it is *not cool*.

Shannon Jade Hughes (11)
Manor Park Community School, Nuneaton

What Is Love?

Love is a game,
Do you know how to play?
It brings big problems in everyone's day,
It ends in disaster, but who do you blame?

Love heart, heartbreak,
Love is a ride,
You should not take!

Love can be bad,
But can always get better.
Most people are glad,
So why not send them a letter?

Nicola Jayne Lenton (11)
Manor Park Community School, Nuneaton

A New School

Starting in Year 7 is a big thing
Cos we're all different in our own way
We help prevent bullying
Like a rhinoceros attacking
Last year the Year 11s got good grades
And they will always be filled with joy
They only tried their hardest
By ditching drugs and alcohol

Now it's our turn to shine!
We have fun at this school
Even though we're all unique.

Heather Jackson (11)
Manor Park Community School, Nuneaton

Is Anybody There?

It was a cold and wet morning,
No one was there!
So I went to school,
No one was there!
I went to form,
No one was there!
So I decided to go home,
No one was there!

No one to care,
From behind, I felt a stare,
Is anyone there, is anyone there?

Alisha Dean (11)
Manor Park Community School, Nuneaton

What's The Point Of Telling?

What's the point in telling the truth, no one seems to believe,
Everyone thinks I spend my time trying to trick and deceive.

I try to tell them once, I try to tell them twice,
But all they say is, 'Lying is not nice!'
No matter how many times I say I am not lying
They never will believe me, so what's the point of trying?

Oh, what's the point of telling the truth when no one seems to believe,
With all this stress I must confess, I'm finding it hard to breathe.

So tell me, what is the point of trying?
Everyone thinks I'm lying!

Lily May Ellis (11)
Manor Park Community School, Nuneaton

I Am Me

I can be the sun, I can be the rain,
I can be the earth, I can be a plain,
I can be anything you want me to be,
But I will always be me!

Leah Crutchlow (12)
Manor Park Community School, Nuneaton

Why Does No One Love Me?

Why does no one love me? I was born to make people happy.
Why does no one love me? I am all by myself.
Why does no one love me? I want to have a friend.
Why does no one love me? I am all by myself.
Why does no one love me? I am really sad and lonely.
Why does no one love me? I am all by myself.
Why does no one love me? I am all by myself.
Why does no one love me? *I want a friend now!*

Someone please love me
I really want a friend *now!*

Dannii Paige Evans (11)
Manor Park Community School, Nuneaton

The Man Who I Called My Dad

He beat me,
He slapped me,
He kicked me on the floor,
He beat me for no reason,
I could take it no more,
I hate him,
I never told him until now,
Four broken bones, three fractured ribs,
He finally stopped,
I slapped him for a change.

Owen Rogers (11)
Manor Park Community School, Nuneaton

Bullying

I'm getting bullied at school
Every day I'm scared
I'm getting abused by people who are older than me
Even outside of school
My teacher doesn't listen to me
I'm scared . . .

Mason Steptoe (12)
Manor Park Community School, Nuneaton

The Road Ahead

Some people may look at me
And say things behind my back
I take it as a compliment
And carry on my track
I think about the road ahead
I think of it as good
I add a smile to my day
Some things may be done
At the end of the day
It's like being stung.

Chelsea Hogarth (13)
Manor Park Community School, Nuneaton

Why Do People Bully Me?

Why do people bully me,
Not only me but other people as well,
I am sick and tired of people bullying me,
Why do they do this?
Do they play violent games or do they take drugs?
Please tell me what you do to be this violent,
Please, please don't hurt me.
Why am I your enemy?
What have I done to upset you?
Please tell me.

Alice Kimberlin (11)
Manor Park Community School, Nuneaton

People

P olite people
E ncouraging people
O rdinary people
P icky people
L arge people
E xciting people.

Kimberley Norton (12)
Manor Park Community School, Nuneaton

I Think Of You

I think of you when I'm running
I think of you when I eat
I think of you every time even in every blink
I think of you when I'm talking
I think of you in my dreams
I think of you when I'm crying so do you think of me?
I put your name in the sand
But the wave took it away
I put your name in the sky but the clouds took it away
I put your name in my heart and forever it will stay.

Arbaz Khalifa Faruk (12)
Manor Park Community School, Nuneaton

He's There, He's There, Or Is He

The silent whisper tells me I'm not alone.
The fire burning down inside my head,
All around me, he's there, he's there.
A headache comes as fast as lightning
And my stomach starts to churn like a swirlpool.
The sky starts to swirl like a tornado
Because that's probably what it is.
He runs like a cheetah and hides like a mouse.
I start to feel bare
Because I know he's there, he's there.

Thomas McIlveen (12)
Manor Park Community School, Nuneaton

What If?

What if there was no fighting?
What if there was no bullying?
What if there were no drugs in school?
What if there was no alcohol?
What if everyone got along?
What if we could get along?

Curtis Atkins (11)
Manor Park Community School, Nuneaton

Feelings Of The Future

Life is such a puzzle
You don't know where to go
You stand up
To get knocked down again.

People always nagging
They are such a pain
Life is one crazy thing
Just like a train . . .

But I don't want it to end!

Ashley Tuck & Leah Crutchlow (12)
Manor Park Community School, Nuneaton

Friends

Friends, friends, friends everywhere
Friends, friends, friends anywhere
Friends cheer you up when you are feeling down
Friends are there when you are getting bullied
Friends need you to stick up for them
Good friends are good and they help you
When you have got homework they will be there
So good friends are nice friends

Good friends will be there.

Chelsea Chamberlain (12)
Manor Park Community School, Nuneaton

Glow-Worm

I'm not dull being a glow-worm,
And I'm never glum,
Because I have a light
Shining out of my bum.

It's fun being a glow-worm,
You have a light
Guide you in the dark.

Lauren Jodie Beech (11)
Manor Park Community School, Nuneaton

My Life

I'm a girl living in a care home,
I have no friends,
I'm always bullied,
It's like having a knife in you,
I don't talk to anyone,
My parents gave me up,
I will never talk to them again,
I hate my life
And I always will.

Paige Smillie Blake (12)
Manor Park Community School, Nuneaton

Anger

Anger will one day overwhelm us,
Anger can involve a death,
Anger causes heartbreak and loss,
Anger turns a good man bad,
Anger upsets people who could lead the way,
Anger is caused by a bad experience,
Anger is inadequate.
Lead people out of the darkness,
I do, so should you.

Liam Jay Perry (11)
Manor Park Community School, Nuneaton

The Finishing Line

I really miss Grandpa and I really don't know why,
I was really upset when I had to say bye.
We had always had fun but how could it happen?
I really loved him but why, why, why?

I'm still a bit upset and now I must admit
He was great, he was cool and he was top of the class
He made my day, I loved him so much,
But now that he's gone, my memories of him *never pass*.

John James Gordon (11)
Manor Park Community School, Nuneaton

Gangsters Crime

All gangsters trying to act cool,
Killing everyone and burning schools,
Then off to the pubs,
For drinks and drugs . . .
Then to bully youngsters to act all hard,
So you can be known as the bully gang Sozzard.
Everything can be solved so . . .
What can we do? . . . Turn around and apologise,
Or tell them to admit their little dirty lies!

Siddiqah Khalifa (12)
Manor Park Community School, Nuneaton

I Wonder

I wonder if we will ever see the point to life,
I wonder if we will ever stop the killing with a knife,
I wonder if we will ever stop the wars,
I wonder if we will ever be a peaceful world.

I wonder if I will ever grow old,
I wonder if I will ever stay as a teen,
I wonder if I will ever have children,
I hope they won't see the world in this state.

Daniel Chandler (11)
Manor Park Community School, Nuneaton

Violence

Hitting and slapping
Punching and kicking
These are the evil things
That go on in streets and alleys
And behind closed doors
Why is the world we live in so violent?
So full of murder, terrorism and fighting.
Will our world's violent problem ever end?

James Wilson (12)
Manor Park Community School, Nuneaton

Feelings

F eelings
E motions
E xpressions
L istening
I mportant
N eglected
G ossip
S ounds.

Mason Holligan (12)
Manor Park Community School, Nuneaton

Football

F it and healthy
O ver reactive
O bedient
T here's always a game on TV
B ullying
A rguments and fights
L iverpool
L earn new skills and tactics.

Callum Twigger (12)
Manor Park Community School, Nuneaton

Stopping The Bullying

Just because I have been bullied,
Don't think you can do it now.
If you do some will say ow!
Why do people always get hurt?
But there is a special person that is called Burt.
One day it got solved
Because he went to the teacher and the teacher sorted it,
Then the person was happy and glad.

Georgia Leech (11)
Manor Park Community School, Nuneaton

Football

F it and healthy all the time
O bedient
O ver reactive
T here's always a bit of fun
B all hogging
A nd arguments and fights in most of the games
L iverpool
L earn new skills all of the time.

Daniel King (12)
Manor Park Community School, Nuneaton

Football

F ree kicks
O ver react
O pposition
T eammates
B uilds up skill
A ggressive sport
L osers always sulk
L ong range shots.

Jordon Blount-Hunt (12)
Manor Park Community School, Nuneaton

Bullies

I feel like thunder
I feel like rain
Every day at school
Is a life of pain
Around school
The bullies always fighting
I wish they could get hit by lightning
I wish, I wish, I wish . . .

Ashley Tuck (12)
Manor Park Community School, Nuneaton

Football

F it and healthy
O wn goal
O ther team is going to win
T here's always a game on TV
B alls going everywhere
A bout to go in
L egends winning the game
L egs moving.

Naeem Ahmedabadi (12)
Manor Park Community School, Nuneaton

Friendship

Friendship is so nice
Friendship you can trust
You have a best friend
You can tell your secrets to
So that you do not have to keep it all in
Friendship you can be happy
Have a friend you can walk around school with
Have a friend you can rely on.

Caitlin Suzanna Lyons (12)
Manor Park Community School, Nuneaton

Friends

F riends are there forever and ever,
R emember they always care,
I n difficult situations they always help you out,
E veryone can be your friend there's no doubt,
N o one will leave you alone,
D on't leave people out of games,
S tick together, they are the only best friends you've got.

Ryan Mceachran (11)
Manor Park Community School, Nuneaton

Friends

Friends, you always need friends
Friends always stick up for you
Friends help you and look after you when you're down
Friends need you just as much as you need them
Friends love you . . . but in a different way to your mum or dad
Friends!

Cara Wallace (12)
Manor Park Community School, Nuneaton

Death Of My Nan

Now I know that you have gone
To the moon, stars and sun,
I know that you were there for me
And you would make me happy.

Life's not fair I have to say
Why did you have to go away?
Lots of love I send to you
Lots of hugs and kisses too,
A photo is all I have to keep
Now that you have gone to sleep.

Things will never be the same now you're gone,
The memories we shared will carry me on,
When I'm feeling sad and blue
I'll just close my eyes and think of you.
I'll miss your smile and your face,
May you rest in a peaceful place.

Lauren Pritchard (13)
Prince Henry's High School, Evesham

Football Is A Game

Football is a game, it does not matter if you do not seem the same.
Tall, short, thin or round football is sound.
When the game kicks off, it all begins.
The fans are all wagging their chins.
As he runs his heart is pounding, when he tackles it is grounding.

As you're running on the ball just as you think you're gonna fall.
You pass it on as a through ball.
You're passed one and passed two.
All is left is the dreaded beachball.

Football is a friendly game with sportsmanship, courage and also fun
But the only problem is kicking racism out of football.

Joseph Robinson (13)
Prince Henry's High School, Evesham

Happiness

Happiness is,
When you're on cloud nine,
Like the brightest star,
That could ever shine.

Happiness is,
When you're feeling fine,
Like a large glass,
Of sparkling wine.

Happiness is,
When you have a good time,
Not when someone,
Commits a terrible crime.

Happiness is,
Like a winding vine,
Some may feel it,
All the time!

Sophie Willmore (11)
St Bede's Catholic Middle School, Redditch

Scary I Am

I am,
the huge spiderweb
inside your old clothes.
The silence,
in the old house.
The angry shark,
who lives in the sea.

I am,
the owl
you see in the dark.
The ghost
who kills people.
The dark
that everyone scares.

I am,
the noise
we hear in the dark.
The angry lion
who lives in the middle of the forest.
The scary ride
in the middle of the park.

I am,
the hairy spider
tickling the sleeping child.
The poisonous snake
who comes in the dark.
The old castle
in the middle of the forest.

Liya Tom (12)
St Bede's Catholic Middle School, Redditch

Confused I Am

I am
The colourless rainbow
Black and white,
The gleaming new battery
That does not work,
The difficult question
With no answer,
The rusty old sign
That points the wrong way,
I am
The scraggy fat cat
That barks,
The weird looking penguin
That lives in a desert,
The fluffy feathered bird
With no wings,
The sat nav
That doesn't know which way to go,
I am
The goal posts
With no net,
A pair of football boots
With no studs,
The brand new set of traffic lights
That flash red, orange and green
And a person in a hall of mirrors.

Confused I am.

Zack Nixon (12)
St Bede's Catholic Middle School, Redditch

I Am

I am
the birthday present
ready to be opened.
A leprechaun that is
happy to find my gold
I am
A jack-in-a-box
ready to pop out.
A picture
ready to be drawn.
I am
An ogre ready to
eat my dinner.
The music ready
to be played.
I am
the brand new pen
ready to be written with.
A book ready
to be read.
I am
the glasses ready
to be worn.
The picture ready
to be taken.

I am happy.

Tammi Richards (12)
St Bede's Catholic Middle School, Redditch

Happy I Ams

I am
A firework
Bursting to fly up high into the sky
A person
Who has just won ninety-two million pounds
A boy and girl
Waiting to eat their sackful of candy.

I am
A poppy
Blooming in the field
A famous painting
Ready to be sold for ten grand
A girl
Waiting for her pink limousine
To come pick her up.

I am
A present
Waiting to be opened
A child
Waiting for Santa to come with
A sackful of presents
A man
Who has just made a world record.

I am happy.

Zoe McGahey (12)
St Bede's Catholic Middle School, Redditch

Human

I feel good, I feel great,
On cloud nine, not on eight,
I feel joyful, ecstatic,
And very dramatic,
I feel happy!

I feel gentle and peaceful,
Slightly humble and bashful,
I feel nervous and modest,
And just, in the oddest,
I feel shy . . .

I feel angry and cross,
Unhappy and great loss,
Wound-up and provoked,
Don't tell me a joke,
I feel . . . *argh!*

I feel low and depressed,
I feel troubled and stressed,
I feel down and blue,
I feel fine (so untrue),
I feel sad.

I am human.

Sara Rafaty (12)
St Bede's Catholic Middle School, Redditch

My Paradise

I lie beneath the warm blue moon,
The sun is yet to awaken,
In the morning wondrous colours shall bloom,
My dark paradise temporarily shaken.

My feelings here are joyous emotions,
I am full of love for this dark sky,
Though I am full of hate for the coming sun,
But all the while, my dark friends will be waiting here
Where I lie.

Grace Down (11)
St Bede's Catholic Middle School, Redditch

The Emotion Roller Coaster

When you are up you are happy,
You are definitely not snappy,
Your smile spreads across your face,
You wouldn't want to be in any other place.

When you go down
Your smile turns into a frown,
You feel rather tragic
Wondering where is the magic

You get a little scared
When you're not prepared
To shoot into a dark hole
Which is as black as coal.

The speed takes you by surprise,
You can't even open your eyes,
Your heart is beating out of your chest,
It's the total opposite of a rest.

Charlie Evans (12)
St Bede's Catholic Middle School, Redditch

I Am . . .

I am the ferocious lion
Hunting its prey,
The bull
That charges at the red flag,
I am the barking dog
Who is aggressive,
The missile
That is about to explode,
I am the monster truck
Crushing all the cars,
The tank
Exploding all the motorbikes

And I am me
And no one can change that.

Daniel Wilkinson (12)
St Bede's Catholic Middle School, Redditch

Happy I Am

I am the beautifully smelling, luscious red roses
in the garden of paradise,
The moist, fertile soil, waiting to be munched through by the worm,
The rainbow-coloured petals on the flower
that everyone has been buying,
I am the gleaming new games console being advertised this second,
The stilettos on celebrity, Angelina Jolie's feet,
The stylish new jeans waiting to be purchased at bargain price,
I am the tyre which is freshly gripped,
The cool, classy convertible roof on the new Mini Cooper,
The 5 litre engine ready for some serious revving,
The brand new skirts on the latest BMW,
I am the brand new textbook on sale now,
The young African child on his first day at school,
The stripy HB pencil that everyone has in their pencil case.

I am happy!

Jack Bowen (12)
St Bede's Catholic Middle School, Redditch

Scared

I am
the cat's eyes
that glow in the dark.
A Chinese dragon
breathing fire.
A hairy spider
dangling over the bed.
I am
the old lady
being followed down an alley.
A child going to school
on his first day
of his lifetime.
I am scared, are you?

Jordon Dance (12)
St Bede's Catholic Middle School, Redditch

Confused I Ams

I am
A word spelt completely wrong
A fire with no flames
A racing car with no wheels
A very valuable antique clock with no hands
A bright green eye that can't see
I am
A complicated maths sum that no one can solve
A brand new book that can't be read
I am
A lovely pink bag with no straps
A beautiful pasta dish with no sauce
A little lost puppy with no real home
An important sign pointing completely the wrong way
A brand new high definition television with no power
I am confused.

Rebecca Hinks (12)
St Bede's Catholic Middle School, Redditch

Confused I Am

I am
The English teacher, who can't read or write
The maths teacher, who can't do algebra
A mom, that can't cook . . . a dad, that can't fix anything
I am
The snow, in the middle of summer
The sun, dark as night
The plant, blue as ink . . . the tree with no leaves or branches
I am
The map, never the right way
The maze, with five exits
The sign, pointing the wrong way . . . the water, you can sit on
I am
The dove, that can't fly
The basketball, that doesn't bounce
The bench, you can't sit on.

Chantelle Maher (12)
St Bede's Catholic Middle School, Redditch

I Am . . .

The person who gives you heart-shaped chocolate
Who broke your little red heart
Who wears your old T-shirts
Red roses that are given to you
Heart that keeps you breathing inside you
Diamond ring on someone's finger
The hug that makes your heart melt
Lipstick tattooed on your cheek
Bullet that stole your heart
Person that holds your hands watching the sunset
Song that makes you happy
The love heart I put on paper

I am in love.

Chelsea Wilkes (12)
St Bede's Catholic Middle School, Redditch

Happy

I am a pair of brand new shoes.
I am beautiful summer's day.
Bright new flowers saying hello
And a little girl shouting peep po!

I am the clown saying funny jokes.
The girl fooling around in the snow.
A boat setting out to sea,
Looking at the fish around me.

I am the girl jumping in the air to the music!
The girl opening pressies on Christmas Day.
I am the butterfly flying in the air.

I am me! *Happy.*

Jade Yarranton (12)
St Bede's Catholic Middle School, Redditch

Objecting

A light flitted gently across
The blue marine bed of aqua.
My face, a shadow, saw lightly
The great moon, a pale reflection.

Ripples danced and ripples grew,
Hair cascading, so much, so much.
Voices! Nothing but a dull thud!
Voices! Echoing, raising more!

Then ropes, singing through metal hoops,
Their singing so much like sirens.
Beams of false light illuminate,
Cut through the home of my own, true peace.

My peace that will soon be broken,
This place of mine soon to be found.
I object, wanting nothing more
Than this watery ignorance.

Objecting, wanting nothing more
Than my grave to be left in peace.

Adele Critchlow (13)
St Philip Howard RC School, Glossop

Footsteps From The Past

Soft blue eyes twinkling in the light,
The dark, black moon, the stars so bright,
The soft, sweet whisper of the owls above,
The silent deserted streets, the harsh known love.
The tall, narrow lamp post, glistening like the sun,
The short, round truth, it had to be done,
The soft, cold scent of the air above,
The long, winding hate, the long-lost love,
The small, kind mumbles of the trees alight,
Walking down the dark path, the gone a fright.
Suddenly I stop there, my footsteps fade.
Looking back at the life that I once made.

Lucy Aspden (13)
St Philip Howard RC School, Glossop

It Is!

It is the thing everyone fears, the torment, the ridicule, the hate
It is the thing that bullies create
It is the thing that keeps you awake
It is the thing that started as a mistake
It is the thing you can't let go
It is the thing that makes you say no
It is bullying.

Jack Swift (13)
St Philip Howard RC School, Glossop

Stop Pollution

P eople think throwing rubbish is a cruelty to wildlife
    and our lives and they're right, don't do it.
O tters trapped in inky seas because of all the pollution ships
    spilling their waste through our oceans. Stop!
L ights turned off will decrease our carbon footprint
    and make the world a better place.
L ead pellets on fishing lines kill our marine life and exotic birds.
U niverse is being affected by greenhouse gases,
    save our generation, take action now.
T reat our world with respect and it will add up.
I t's your turn to help our planet, try something positive,
    make a difference.
O xygen we take for granted we can't see it,
    but we need it, don't pollute it.
N ever turn the Earth into our dustbin,
    three tips why and what to do; clean it, help it, need it.

Iris Hawkins (11)
Springwell Community School, Chesterfield

Cruelty

Just imagine walking, walking down a lane full of cold-hearted people,
Who poach endangered animals for their fur and meat
And have the mind to leave animals outside
in the cold, crisp, dark night
To freeze and starve to death alone . . .

Animal testing is another, leaving them to suffer in pain,
As you watch them whilst they do harmful,
life-threatening experiments on them!
Would you do something or nothing?

Would you laugh if you saw hunters poaching a white lion on TV?
Would you laugh if you saw them kill a helpless kitten
whilst doing some experiment on it?

Look through the eyes of a helpless animal like these for once!

Join me! Go against animal cruelty!

Paige Holmes (11)
Springwell Community School, Chesterfield

Crime Busting

Teams of gangsters roaming around
They are making a massive heap of sound
They make crime all the time
That's why I'm writing this rhyme
While we still have the time
The bigger the crime
The longer the time
They go on and run away
No one will ever see them again
They get very flustered
Because they will always get busted
So if you see any crime
Go on and call 999 whilst you still have time.

Liam Deane (11)
Springwell Community School, Chesterfield

Our World

Pollution in the sea is really affecting me.
Rubbish everywhere I look even in the streets.
A tear runs down my face what's happening to this place?
What's happening to our world?
It's really very sad.
Never knew things could get this bad.
It's down to us to sort,
That's all we need to do.
So next time you see some litter you know just what to do.
It'll only take one minute, that's not a lot of time.
Just think, it's our world you're saving.
It's the most important thing.
Our world, our lives, our future, *bin it!*

Olivia Bulley (11)
Springwell Community School, Chesterfield

Leave Me Alone

Leave me alone, I've had enough,
I'm tired of feeling alone,
Why did you have to push me over
And break my mobile phone?

Leave me alone, I wish you would stop,
You're making me feel sad,
When you call me names and kick me,
Why do you have to be so bad?

Leave me alone, just walk away,
You have no right to tease,
I've never done anything to hurt you
So I'm asking you to stop it please.

Ben Carley (11)
Springwell Community School, Chesterfield

Crime

Gun crime, car crime is all very bad,
People are crying for the children they once had,
Crime is in the air morning till night,
Why oh why do they have to fight?

Why can't they stop?
Why do they kill?
What about the families
Whose place they will never fill?

They don't care at the time,
About doing the crime,
About the effect it has on loved ones,
When they play about with handguns.

Amy Turner (12)
Springwell Community School, Chesterfield

A Nightmare To Remember

You lie in bed
With your ted
Crying, rocking
With your clock tick-tocking.

As you fall asleep
Nothing will creep
As you cry a tear
There is nothing to fear.

You toss and turn
Your tummy does churn
To wake in the morning
You find your mum mourning.

Katie Milner (11)
Springwell Community School, Chesterfield

Wind And Rain

The wind begins to howl
And the trees begin to sway
The clouds begin to gather
The rain is on the way
But not in gushes, but down gently it comes.
The start of a miserable day becomes
I sit at my window hearing as it falls
The rain pattering on my patio doors
Looks like the rain is going away
Yeah tomorrow looks like a lovely day
But don't be so sure my mother said
Tomorrow is a brand new day.

Esme Jones (11)
Springwell Community School, Chesterfield

My Family

I have many things, all on my mind, trouble everywhere,
I think you might find.
Trouble at home, trouble at school, nothing right,
I'm just a fool.
My mum and dad, they're divorced,
My brother, he's in the Air Force.
Nine weeks, he's going to be gone,
He's been there for me,
Since I was one.
Nothing's right, but I guess I can say,
My family are great and together we'll stay.

Kate Plowman (13)
Springwell Community School, Chesterfield

When Will? Why Do?

When will teenagers stop doing things wrong?
When will they stop thinking they're cool cos of what's in their hand?
Why do they fight for no reason given?
They know they won't go to Heaven.
Why do people think they're cool cos of their gang?
When will they know that a record ain't good?
When will they think about others instead?
Cos their parents are worried about if they're dead?
Don't think about yourself all the time!
When you get killed is what you call *crime!*

Megan Lilley (13)
Springwell Community School, Chesterfield

Family Love

My mum makes me happy
She lets me play on the Xbox
My sister says no
My dad makes me angry
He's always on about my feet
My sister makes me happy
When she's not around
But they're my family
That's why I love them.

Benjamin Hall (13)
Springwell Community School, Chesterfield

Friends

Friends are people who stick up for you.
Friends are people who care for you.
Friends are people who you should trust.
Friends are people who help you.
Friends are people who love you.
Friends are some of the most important people in your life.
That's why friends are in everyone's life.

Lee-Anne Longmore (13)
Springwell Community School, Chesterfield

Brothers And Sisters

Brothers and sisters always make you angry
Brothers and sisters always get on your nerves
Brothers and sisters always get you grounded
Brothers and sisters always embarrass you
Brothers and sisters are not always fair
Brothers and sisters sometimes make you feel unhappy
Brothers and sisters always get the priority
Brothers and sisters always get the attention
But secretly brothers and sisters always make us happy.

Ryan Smith (13)
Springwell Community School, Chesterfield

The Weekend

The weekend is here, jump up and cheer
Time for chocolate, time for sweets
Time for midnight, telly and Coronation Street
Here's the jelly, here's the drink
Listening to some music, an artist named Pink
I'm on my laptop talking to Jack
I've got to go now, I'm going to pack
I'm going on holiday, it's the weekend
Jump up and cheer, the weekend is here!

Ellie May Palmer (13)
Springwell Community School, Chesterfield

Call Me A Name

When they call me names they're all the same
They pick on a spot and pick on it a lot

Just cos I cannot see
Doesn't make me not good or who I try to be
But the bullies don't see the good side of me

It makes me mad and sometimes sad
When they pick on me cos I can't see.

Carl Jabes Leadbeater (13)
Springwell Community School, Chesterfield

Racism

Why do we call them names
And not involve them in our games?
Sometimes people can be so lame.
Everyone is the same.

Why can't people play together,
And be friends forever?
And don't fight ever.
Even if it's stormy weather.

Just because you're black or white
Means we still have the same eyesight
So try your best not to fight
In the middle of the night.

Involve people with what you do
Or even invite them in for a stew
The actions you take and the things you do
Could make our world brand new.

The world is beginning to shake
It is turning into an earthquake
Learn from your mistake
And try to give and not just take!

Joshua Messer (13)
Swanwick School & Sports College, Swanwick

Stealing

Gigi likes to steal jewels
They are her favourite tools
Gigi should watch out!
There are spy cameras about
Gigi, the police are on their way
What are you going to say?
Gigi you're now in court
The lesson you have been taught
Gigi now you're free
Good is now what you must be.

Eva Shepherd (12)
Swanwick School & Sports College, Swanwick

Guns And Knives

Just because my brother carries a gun,
Just because he likes to have fun,
Just because he likes to fight,
Just because he might ignite,
Just because he looks scary and mean
doesn't mean he functions like a machine.
Just because he carries a knife
doesn't mean he is going to take a life.
Just because he wears a hoodie
doesn't mean he isn't a goodie.
Just because he wears dark clothes
might mean he is trying to pose.
Just because teenagers are loud
doesn't mean they are not proud.
Just because teenagers can get mad
that doesn't mean we are all bad.
Just because we sometimes make mistakes
it doesn't mean you have to hate.
Just give a chance and try to listen,
I promise you we are all on the same positive mission!

Keiran Daken (14)
Swanwick School & Sports College, Swanwick

It Isn't Fair

It isn't fair to call people on their colour
It isn't fair to call people on the way they talk
It isn't fair to laugh at people because of their religion
It isn't fair to bully people that come from a different place
It isn't fair to insult a person who wears a turban
It isn't fair to mock someone who wears different clothes
It isn't fair to point at someone who wears a religious mark
You can stop it!
You can tell your friends not to point
You can tell someone, 'Don't stare'
You can say to someone, they are not hard to mock them
You can tell everyone, 'They're the same as you and me.'

David Beavan (14)
Swanwick School & Sports College, Swanwick

Young Writers Information

We hope you have enjoyed reading this book - and that you will continue to enjoy it in the coming years.

If you like reading and writing poetry drop us a line, or give us a call, and we'll send you a free information pack.

Alternatively if you would like to order further copies of this book or any of our other titles, then please give us a call or log onto our website at www.youngwriters.co.uk

Young Writers Information
Remus House
Coltsfoot Drive
Peterborough
PE2 9JX
(01733) 890066